RV Living:

The RVing Lifestyle:
Start Your Motorhome Adventure!

+

RV Travel: *Your Guide to a Full-Time Nomad Life / RV Retirement. Start Traveling, Camping and Boondocking as an RVer!*

(2 books in 1)

Michael Van Brown

publisher for any reparation, damages, or monetary loss due to the information herein, either directly or indirectly.

Respective authors own all copyrights not held by the publisher.

The information herein is offered for informational purposes solely and is universal as so. The presentation of the information is without contract or any type of guarantee assurance.
The trademarks that are used are without any consent, and the publication of the trademark is without permission or backing by the trademark owner. All trademarks and brands within this book are for clarifying purposes only and are owned by the owners themselves, not affiliated with this document.

Table of Contents:

RVing Lifestyle:

Start Your Motorhome Adventure!

Michael Van Brown

Introduction

Hello and welcome to your greatest adventure yet! Have you always dreamed of the freedom that comes with being on the open road? Traveling from one location to the next, waking up to new and exciting views every day? Wouldn't it be exciting if every day could be a new adventure? It most certainly can be, when you're living on the road full time in an RV.

If you're thinking about buying your very first RV, you've come to the right place. *RV Living* is going to be your very own personal guide that is going to walk you through everything you need to know to prepare to become a full-time nomad. There's a lot more than goes into owning an RV than most people realize, especially where the legal considerations are concerned.

The unbiased information you're going to encounter in the following chapters is going to leave you with all the details that you need to make an informed decision and better prepare you for your upcoming adventure on the road:

RVing Lifestyle: Start Your Motorhome Adventure!, in fact, is the essential guide packed full with all the information you need to make a decision about what it's going to be like leaving behind most of your worldly possessions, selling your home and getting on the road with nothing more than several wells thought out plans and a sense of adventure.

Covering all the basics which include how to deal with the emotions that come with leaving everything you know behind, easy ways to get rid of your stuff, the pros and cons of this life, how to make the perfect financial plan, money saving tips, which motorhome is the right one for you and more! Everything you need to begin the first phase of your journey is right here.

There are plenty of books on this subject on the market, thanks again for choosing this one! Every effort was made to ensure it is full of as much useful information as possible, please enjoy!

Chapter 1: Start an Amazing Journey

Life on the road can be one of the greatest adventures you've ever embarked on. You haven't had a taste of what ultimate freedom feels like until you have lived in an RV. The ability to travel anywhere you want, wake up every day in a new location, explore places that most people will never get to see in their lifetime. That is absolute bliss for those with the wanderlust spirit within them.

RVing And the Emotions That Come With It

You can plan and prepare and cover every inch of the entire process until you're blue in the face, but you may still never be fully prepared for the emotions that are going to come with uprooting your life as you know it. Going on an RV adventure for a short holiday stint is going to be *very different* from that of living on the road full time. No matter how much you prepare yourself for what's to come, when those wave of emotions finally start to hit, they can hit hard.

As you're about to hit the open road, questions start niggling at the back of your mind. Are you doing the right thing? Is this the best decision for you? What about your family? Is this going to work out? What if you don't like it? What if you realized halfway through that this might have been a mistake? There'll be plenty of "what ifs" to ponder along the way. It's a big change you're about to make if you're thinking of living on the road full time. It's going to be unlike anything you've ever experienced before this, you're bound to have questions and concerns along the way. Making the big announcement to your family and friends about what you're going to do, they're going to have *even more concerns, questions, fears, worries and doubts* piled onto your existing ones. Several times along the way you're going to stop to consider what on earth you're doing leaving a comfortable home for the great unknown.

Being wrought with emotions is a normal process that any first-time RVer especially is going to need to overcome, and the best way to do that is to prepare yourself for what's ahead and carve out coping mechanisms to help you get through it.

- **Emotional Moment #1 - Leaving Your Home, Family and Your Friends.** Saying goodbye to the ones we love is never easy, even if it is for a short period of time. Going on a short holiday is completely different because you know exactly when you're going to return. If you're embarking on this RV journey full time, you don't know when the next time you're going to be able to see them next. The emotions that you're going to feel will depend on how close of a relationship you have with your family and friends. The closer you are, the harder it's going to be for you to leave. As hard as it may think, try to focus on the positives that lie ahead and why you chose to begin this journey in the first place. Let your family and friends know you're going to keep in touch as often as you can. Phone calls, Skype calls, FaceTime, emails, texts, technology has made it exceedingly easy for us to stay connected no matter where in the world we are.

- **Emotional Moment #2 - Saying Goodbye To The Familiar**

Community. If you've been staying at the current home you have for a significant amount of time, you're likely to have formed a sense of kinship with the community you live in. Your doctor, hairdresser, trainer at the gym, the local grocer who greets you with the smile, it doesn't quite hit you that you're going to miss this sense of familiarity until you're about to leave for real. You're going to miss the familiar neighborhood, how easy it is to get around because you know exactly where to go, the usual daily routine you've become so used to over the years. The emotions that you feel may not be as strong as the ones you have for your family and friends, but some people might still feel a little upset at the notion of having to say goodbye to their comfort zone. It's the little things that we take for granted every day that we end up missing the most.

- **Emotional Moment #3 - Saying Goodbye To Your Home.** Hitting the RV life as a full-timer, one of the biggest considerations you're going to have is about selling your home. If you're serious about living on the road full-time, it only makes sense to give up your home since you won't be around anymore to appreciate it. Selling a home for anyone is an emotional process. All this time, you worked hard because it was your life's goal to get a good job and a good home for your family. Now, you're about to sell your comfortable home for a mobile home on wheels. It's a big change. Your home has been your sanctuary all these years, the one place you knew you would always be safe, and now you're about to give it up for the great unknown. It's going to be painful to part with those memories, but think about all the reasons why you decided to do this to help you get through the process.

- **Emotional Moment #4 - Getting Rid of Your Stuff.** especially in today's modern materialistic society, the biggest hurdle for many people to wrap their minds around is the idea of getting rid of stuff! Look around you right now. What do you see?

You might be reading this in a living room filled with furniture like a TV, couches, recliners, a couple of tables, décor on the walls and on a coffee table, books and magazines stacked on a bookshelf, etc.

Now, go into your kitchen area. In your kitchen, you might have anywhere from two to ten appliances that you use on a daily or weekly basis, food stored in a nice big fridge and in cabinets (much of which will go bad before you even use it, if you're like me!).

What type of bed do you enjoy sleeping in every night? Do you have a nice big king or queen-size mattress and a little end table filled with reading material and a nice big dresser filled with clothes you've collected for years and a closet filled with clothes for any imaginable occasion? How about shoes? (Ladies, take a breath.) Can you imagine downsizing your shoe collection to just a couple of pairs?

If just the thought of getting rid of your stuff makes your stomach churn a bit, you're not alone. But don't let that stop you from looking further into the process.

There are actually a lot of things you can learn and tools you can utilize to make the process easier. Perhaps a good starting point is to think about what you might be giving up for the sake of holding on to all that stuff. How much of your stuff is actually important to you versus habitual attachment? What would it take for you to let go of some of that nice furniture? Would you trade your sofa for a view of one of the most beautiful national parks in the US for a week or a month? Oftentimes, we don't realize it, but that feeling of attachment to material things is formed out of habit and comfort. We don't really need all of those items clogging up our closets, but they make up a portion of what we consider home, and so their importance might feel bigger than what they actually merit. If you're really serious about this RV thing, odds are, you're prepared to put a little effort into learning to let of things for what you believe you can get out of an RV experience.

So what exactly am I talking about here when I speak of the tradeoff? Well, let's start with some big picture things.

There is a movement going on right now toward the concept of minimalism and how living a minimalist lifestyle can improve a person's life in many ways. When I talk to other RV-ers about the beginning stages of preparing for RV life, many of them talk about the nerves they felt about getting rid of their stuff, but then most of them express how freeing it felt to unburden themselves of that same stuff that had trapped them in the first place.

One of the big impetuses for moving to an RV lifestyle is freedom, right? You will be amazed at how much freedom you will experience from just lightening the load of things weighing you down in one spot. If you're itching to get away, then this is just one of the necessary steps to getting there. But there is a lot more to consider here. You have more options than you think when it comes to downsizing to get ready to live in an RV. If you have items in your life that you simply can't part with, consider having a storage facility to keep these items while you are on the road. Alternatively, you can hand over these things to friends and family members for safekeeping. You might have big photo albums or framed pictures that are precious to you but that you know you won't have room for in the RV. That's perfectly understandable. You might have a precious record collection you've created over the course of your lifetime, or some other collection that you decide you don't want to part with. All we're talking about here is rearranging the stuff in your life to be conducive with full-time RV living. You don't have to trash or donate every single thing in your home. We will talk better about this later.

- **Emotional Moment #5 - Leaving Life As You Know It.** You're about to leave behind what is considered a "traditional" way of life and trading it in for a full-time life on the road. With this emotional scenario, what you're likely to be feeling is fear rather than sadness. Here's where all those doubts, fears and worries are going to spring up again and make you wonder what on earth were you thinking, or are you really doing this, are you making the right choice. Until you get behind the wheel and start your first drive, you're going to experience several moments when second thoughts are going to tempt you to throw in the towel and give up on your dream. In the face of second thoughts, it can be hard to remember why you wanted to do this, so try your best to keep your heart and your mind open, and think about all the adventures that lie ahead waiting for you. The different places you'll see, new people to meet, new experiences and endless possibilities.

Leaving, in the beginning, is always hard, but you are so much stronger than you know. Emotions come and go, there will be many moments where you experience ups and downs along the way. Give yourself some time to adjust to life on the road, and once those new experiences start kicking in, the sadness will slowly fade away over time.

Living On the Road

Living on the road is going to be a different experience for everyone. Some absolutely revel in the sheer exhilaration that comes with the freedom of the open road. Others experience more ups and downs. For some, the sense of adventure kicks in almost immediately, while others may take a while for it to sink in.

Whether you've recently quit and left your job in favor of the nomad lifestyle, or you've retired, the RV life is going to be an experience that forever changes your life. Making all the preparations and buying your first RV is just the beginning. What comes next, though? What is to be expected from living on the road full-time?

Hitting the road solo, or with your family and a couple of pets in tow, here's what every first-timer should prepare for:

- Familiarizing yourself with your RV
- Plan, prepare and research your destinations
- Make a checklist before heading out
- Sort out your insurance and domicile
- Downsize your belongings and learn to live like a minimalist
- Communicate regularly
- Keep an open mind and be flexible
- Prepare for the unexpected
- Enjoy the experience

Once Again, as you'll see, one of the biggest adjustments you'll need to get used to is downsizing your belongings. On the road, you're not going to need half of the stuff that you *think* you will. Only the essentials which are needed to survive comfortably should be brought along with you, and everything else is going to have to go.

When it comes to RV living, less is definitely more. The less stuff you bring along with you, the freer you'll be to move around quickly and efficiently. Remember, you're not going to be staying in one place for very long as you would with a home, there's going to be a lot of packing to do which could delay your trips if you bring far too much stuff with you.

Feeling the Freedom of Just You and Your RV

This is the ultimate stress-free lifestyle. Maybe not *entirely* stress-free since there are bound of be a few bumps and challenges along the way, but certainly a lot more stress-free than a life confined to a 9 to 5 job where all you do is just work to pay the bills. RV living has been described as the ultimate life of freedom because you have complete control over where you go, how long you remain in one location, where you're going to set up camp next, how much time you spend driving on the road, how much time you allocate to exploring a location, and even how much money you're going to make while you're on your travels. This is the freedom that so many are yearning for, and the RV is the answer to that prayer.

Previously, full-time RVers consisted of mainly those who had already retired. However, things are very different today as more younger people are giving up the traditional life in favor of the nomadic one. Thanks to technology, it is easier than ever to work while you're on the go, as long as you've got a laptop and a good internet connection, and making money to support themselves while they live on the road has made RV living full time a very viable option for anyone who wants to do it.

Then there is the concept of "workamping" (work and camping) which has made full-time RV living even more viable for all age groups. At the same time, workamping has made it possible for RVers to survive on a much lower income since they get a free place to park which often comes with free WiFi, water and electricity too. In exchange, the RVer works anywhere from 17 to 20 hours a week, and in some cases, they receive a paycheck too. This has allowed many RVers to significantly trim down their expenses without compromising too much on the quality of life. For those who don't like the redundancy of a strict routine, this arrangement works out well for them since most workamper jobs are seasonal, which means you could be doing a different job every couple of months.

Sorry, but I have to repeat this: another thing which contributes to more young people starting to pick up on the RV way of life is the realization that they don't need so many material possessions in their life to make them happy. Why continue spending almost every penny that they earn accumulating even more stuff they don't need when that same amount could be used to fund their travels and experiences instead? The rat race is never-ending and combined that with the office politics and the stress of the job, only to have that income go towards making payment after payment, suddenly life on the road seems like a much better option. Think about it, would you rather have more stuff in your home which doesn't bring you the joy or happiness you thought it would? Or a life of freedom of the open road with priceless experiences that money can't buy? Would you rather wake up each day dreading the daily commute to work? Or wake up every morning with a smile on your face wondering what new adventure awaits and where you're heading off to next?

Sure, there are some things you might have to sacrifice to live this life, but we are making sacrifices and compromises anyway. Why not do it for something that is worthwhile this time? RVers who have given up the traditional life have never been happier because they're *doing something that makes them happy.* That's the difference.

Experiences are priceless and you've got two options to choose from. You can either choose to read about it on the Internet and live vicariously through others, wishing that it could be you. Or you could do something about it and actually go out and live your life. You are going to grow and change so much from the person you were before you started this adventure. Every encounter is going to leave an impact on you, teach you something new, whether it's good or bad. There's no one can say they haven't returned from their RV journey a changed person.

When you live on the road, every day feels like a vacation. The world is yours for the taking, and each day brings a brand new beginning. Traveling across the country, living out your dream, that's freedom.

Easy Ways to Get Rid of Your Stuff

A challenge everyone who plans to live in their RV full-time is going to face is what to do with all their stuff. If you're family and friends don't mind helping you out and storing some of your stuff away, that's great! But if you don't you're going to need to find easy ways to get rid of your stuff because there's going to be *a lot of work* involved.

Even though you know that almost everything must go, it's still going to be a bittersweet experience, and very time consuming one too, depending on how much stuff you have.

Thinking and deciding about what items you should keep and which to donate or trash is not a job that's going to get done in a day. A lot of your belongings are going to mean something to you, and if you could hold onto them, you would like to (think relatives and friends again). For the items that you do want to sell and get rid, here's what you could do with them:

- **Sell Them on Craigslist** - This is perfect for big-ticket items like your beds, sofas, other furniture and even your car. A pro with this approach is that Craigslist has a large community, and depending on where you live, your stuff could sell very quickly. Plus it is easy to use, all you need is a short description, a couple of good quality photos, name your price and state your location. The more detailed your description and your photos are, the quicker your stuff is going to sell. One downside to Craigslist though are the scammers, so exercise some caution when it comes to your personal information.

- **Selling On Facebook -** Why not put the world's most widely used and popular social media platform to good use to help you sell your stuff quickly. You could post your items for sale on your personal Facebook page in case any of your connections are interested in them, and post them on community pages or groups as well who are on the lookout for good quality second-hand items. The pro with this platform is its wide reach, and if you end up selling to one of your contacts, they're bound to be a lot more reliable and trustworthy than scammers.

- **Holding a Garage Sale -** This probably might not be an option if you live in an apartment, but if you do own a home, a garage sale is another quick and easy way to unload your stuff onto your neighbor's or anyone else looking for a bargain.

- **Donating to Goodwill -** Goodwill and Salvation Army are great options for the stuff that you want to donate. At least you know your stuff will be going to someone who is in need of them, and that might help to make you feel better about parting with your possessions.

- **VarageSale -** An online community where you can buy and sell your items safely, you'll be able to buy and sell almost anything on this platform. If buying and selling safely is a huge concern for you, VarageSale transacts with other people who are verified buyers or sellers in your neighborhood.

- **eBay -** Another online platform which is a favorite for those looking to sell new or used items. eBay's approach is auction based, so buyers can come and bid on the items that they like, which means your stuff has the potential to earn more from the initial asking price you published.

Still can't quite bring yourself to say goodbye? Don't worry, you're not the only one. Make the process a little easier on yourself by detaching yourself from your items before you start putting them up for sale. You know that you're doing this for a reason, and you now need to make a commitment to giving up all the unnecessary for something even greater. You're only going to miss these items in the beginning because you're so used to having them, but once you hit the road, it'll dawn on you that you're not going to miss these things much at all. Who knows? You might not even remember half the stuff you've sold off after a while.

Another tip to make the process easier is to think about selling early and selling as often as you can. To give yourself time to wait for the best deals and offers on items that you know still have value, think about selling as early as a couple of months before your intended departure date. Not all your items are going to sell quickly, and you don't want to be rushing at the last minute and stressed out that a lot of your items haven't sold yet. Put your items up for sale one after another whenever you've got the time to spare to write up a great description about it. Set aside sometime during the weekends to start pricing and sorting your items.

The Pros and Cons of the RV Life

Not everyone may be taken the idea of having a home on wheels at the start. Giving up the standard American dream home in favor of a smaller, more compact and mobile option doesn't seem to make much sense. Why would anyone even consider such a thing and choose an RV over a home? Well, for one very simple reason - *the adventure.* Admittedly, like everything else, there are going to be some pros and cons to the scenario, but for those who can't ignore the call to freedom any longer, the cons are a small price to pay.

The pros that you can expect living in an RV full-time include:

- **A Different View Every Day** - Imagine waking up every morning and being greeted by a different scenery? Imagine your view not being one of crowds and traffic jams as everyone jostles about trying to make it work on time. One day, you could be waking up to a spectacular view of the ocean, and another day you could be greeted by the majestic view of the mountains when you step outside your RV door.

- **Goodbye Mortgages** - No home, no mortgage. No more gigantic debt looming over you that you constantly have to keep diverting your hard earned cash towards. No more giant debt sucking out a huge chunk of your monthly income. Paying off debt can be soul-crushing, and that is one of the biggest pros of living a simple life on the road. You're free from one of the biggest debts which tie homeowners down for years.

- **Goodbye Rent -** If you're not a homeowner, then a good chunk of your earnings was going towards your rent. No home to rent means more money to be saved. With the prices of rent the way they are these days, RV living is suddenly looking like a much better option. At least you know you wouldn't be forced to pay an absurd amount of money to live in a tiny room in the city.

- **Developing A Deeper Sense of Gratitude -** When you spend time on the road, living with only the bare essentials and communicating with loved ones is a luxury, you start to develop a deeper sense of gratitude for the little things in life. Things that were so easy to take for granted in the past, like having good WiFi, or being able to catch up with your family and friends over a meal whenever you liked. Having a nice big bathroom with a hot shower every day. The little luxuries that have become so much a part of our life and we don't miss until they're gone. It's hard to become more appreciative of what you have when you only live with the bare essentials.

- **Free Entertainment** - Instead of paying money for entertainment each month, you now get to enjoy it for free by being outdoors and exploring all that nature has to offer. Instead of paying a monthly bill to Netflix and chill on your sofa, developing an unhealthy sedentary habit, your entertainment now lies outdoors. A hike up the mountain getting some fresh air and exercise won't cost you a dime. A swim in the ocean can be done for free, along with soaking up the sun as you relax by the beach. When the weather is perfect for long walks outdoors, exploring your surroundings beats sitting on the sofa binge-watching TV shows for hours.

- **Endless Possibilities** - Everyday can feel like an adventure when you never know what's waiting for you at the next destination. The people you'll meet, things to see and explore, the excitement of not knowing what the next stop is going to bring is part of the magic of living a nomadic life.

- **Cleaning Just Got Easier** - If cleaning has never been your forte, then you'll love living in an RV. A smaller space means quicker cleaning time, and you'll even start to clean as you go because the dirty dishes in the sink simply can't be ignored when there's no place to run.

- **Save Money on Hotels -** Who needs a hotel when you're literally bringing your home with you everywhere that you go? That's the beauty about living in an RV, you've got everything you need at every destination and you don't have to shell out a fortune on hotels or Airbnb accommodations.

Now that you've covered all the perks that come with RV living, it's time to look at some of the downsides to living on a home on wheels:

- **No Escaping Traffic -** You might have been able to avoid the traffic rush to work, but being on the road as much as you will when you live in an RV full time means that there are going to be moments when you simply can't avoid being caught in a jam. You might have to be prepared to be stuck in traffic for hours at times, a definite downside which could cause significant delays to your next pit stop.

- **Fuel Is Expensive -** The price of fuel is another downside to going mobile 24/7. You may have saved on expenses in several other areas, but there's no escaping the hefty price tag which comes with having to fuel up your home when you're on the go. Getting stuck in traffic means you're burning more fuel than what you might have initially budgeted. Always good to have some spare funds on hand in cases of unexpected emergencies like these.

- **Feeling Cramped -** If you're not journeying alone, it can feel like you're constantly getting in each other's way a lot because of the cramped and limited space you have to work with. Private time alone is another luxury you're going to have to forgo unless you're RVing alone that is. It can start to feel a little cramped since all spaces within the RV are going to be significantly smaller than what you're used to.

- **Sticking to Budgets Can Be Tricky -** When you're on the go and anything might happen, it can sometimes be a challenge to stick to the budget you so carefully planned and prepared for. Sure, you may have budgeted for emergencies, but you still would have liked to hold onto that cash if you could.

- **Limited Contact -** You might have to get used to the idea that you'll only be able to contact your family when there's a good WiFi connection or cell service. Definitely won't be as frequent as what you might have done before when you were living in the city or town. Everything's going to rely on good cell service and internet connection now.

Generally speaking, as you already know, picking up and leaving to live full-time in an RV means leaving all of your familiar surroundings, including the people you used to see on a regular basis. But this will be a harder transition for some people than others depending on the people in one's life and where they are located, of course. If you are getting ready to retire and your kids live in different parts of the country, it may actually be a great thing for you to go on the road full-time because you have the opportunity to go see your kids on your own schedule. Perhaps one of your kids lives in Texas and the other in Tennessee. You can pick up and go spend a month near one kid, then go travel to Tennessee and spend another month or two in this area. If you were living in your old home, you would have to plan and spend hundreds of dollars on plane tickets, renting a car, etc., in order to go see your kids.

As I said, each situation will be different in this regard. Though you may be traveling with an amazing partner, you may find it a strange thing to suddenly not be able to pick up and go meet a girlfriend at your favorite coffee shop downtown or go to your favorite bookshop after work. We tend to take things like this for granted until they are gone.

- **Disposing Of Your Own Sewage -** Probably one of the grossest things most people would find about RV living is having to dispose of your own sewage. Not to mention that the sewage tank is literally going to be going along with you everywhere that you go since it's right underneath the RV toilet. The idea of having to handle your own excrement can be a major put off for many.

- **No Hot Water On Demand -** Another household luxury to say goodbye to is having hot water anytime you want. With no permanent heater, it can sometimes take a while for the water tank to warm up, so hot showers are not going to be instant anytime you like anymore.

Chapter 2: Make a Perfect Plan

Ready to hit the wide open road? Not just yet, there's a couple of things that need to be sorted out first, like figuring out the cost of living in an RV, having a proper financial and logistics plan, what equipment is needed to live on the road as full-time RVer.

Creating the Perfect Financial and Logistical Plan

Are your finances ready for RV life? You might be, but your finances need to be as prepared as you are. The last thing you want is to be stranded somewhere unable to move around due to financial constraints. Before you get behind the wheel and take off, you need to first take a good, long look at your finances, and then make a list of what expenses you can expect to incur while you're on the move.

There are a couple of other questions which need to be addressed when you're creating your financial plan:

- How do you intend to finance your RV purchase? If you aren't financing your RV purchase on your own, some cash needs to be allocated aside each month for the loan repayments.
- What are the other bills you expect to incur on the road?
- How much do you intend to budget to survive the month aside from your bill payments? This will fluctuate depending on whether you plan to live in your RV long-term or for a short period. Going on

the road permanently is going to require a much bigger budget of course.

This may seem obvious but creating your financial plan is going to be a very personal approach. Your budget, for example, is not going to be the same as another Rvers because you might have different lifestyles. Some Rvers have more leeway when it comes to spending, while others prefer to stick to a strict budget and not deviate too much from it. The financial plan needs to be realistic and suitable for your needs. The same thing goes with your logistics plan.

Living in an RV is going to require some adjustments to be made. Sometimes you might have to make *a lot* of adjustments, especially budget wise. You're not going to be able to spend like you used to anymore since you're not going to be living the same way. Most likely you're going to be doing seasonal jobs or freelance work instead of having a steady paycheck coming in each month, so being carefree with your spending may not be such a viable option anymore.

You may have been able to get by each month without a proper budget or some sort of financial plan in place, but when you're living full-time in an RV, things are different. Your routine isn't going to be fixed, unexpected situations are more likely to crop up, and a logistics plan becomes a must to map out your journey as efficiently as possible to save money.

Let's take a look at some of the expenses you can expect and what should be included in your financial plan as you prepare to map one out:

- **Cost of RV** – This is going to be by far your biggest expense if you're not financing it on your own. It is significantly cheaper than owning a home, but it still comes with a pretty hefty price tag. If you're taking a loan out to purchase your RV, your biggest expense every month is going to be the loan repayments. Your financial plan needs to include not just the cost of purchasing the RV, but the insurance, vehicle registration, licenses that may be required maintenance and fuel included too. Deciding on how much you can afford and what you'd be willing to spend will help you later on as you narrow down the choices of the kind of RV you should purchase.

- **Miscellaneous RV Costs** – Other costs associated with living in an RV include the cost of your extended warranty, towing insurance, RV club dues, road assistance membership, and security system (if any).

- **Running RV Costs** – This includes your gas or diesel costs, propane, upgrades, maintenance and repair, campsite rental, overnight costs, supplies and tools (because you're going to need to DIY your own repairs a lot when you're on the road), and dump station fees.

- **Daily Living Expenses** – Groceries, internet, mobile phone bills, household items you may need, miscellaneous food costs (if you decide to order takeaway or fast food once in a while), laundry, clothing, toiletries, entertainment or recreation costs, pet supplies (if any).

- **Emergency Fund** – A cash fund set aside in case of any emergencies.

Planning your budget is going to be a very individual thing, and no two budgets are going to be exactly the same. As long as you've got some cash set aside in case of an emergency, you should be fine. When you're on the move as much as you will be, sometimes there may not be an ATM or bank immediately handy, so it's a good idea to keep a little bit of cash on hand just in case you might need it. Anything could happen at any time, and it's always better to be prepared for any situation.

When you're crunching the numbers and looking at the feasibility of your current financial state, you might find that your numbers are in the negative and you're not as financially prepared as you initially thought. That's okay, tackle the process in stages, and start by reviewing your financial plan and see what other adjustments can be made. Handling the process in stages buys you more time to get your finances well and truly prepared before you make the transition to living in an RV.

Tips to Save Money on the Road

Living without a steady paycheck can make you break out into a nervous sweat when you're doing this for the first time. Luckily, there a couple of savvy ways that Rvers can trim their expenses to save some money:

- **Budgets** – They're there for a reason, and if there ever was a time you needed to stick to a budget, Rving would be it. Managing your money well is the key to stretching out your dollars, even more so when you don't have a full-time income to depend on. Develop good budget habits to help you stay on top of your spending, and maybe even save some money too.

- **Change Your Financial Habits** – A little change can go a long way financially. Spend only on what you *need* and know exactly where your money is going, will help you to curb a lot of unnecessary spending you might have been prone to in the past. Before making each purchase, ask yourself if this is a necessity. If it isn't, you could probably do without it.

- **Search for Free Parking** – Whenever possible find places to park for free so you avoid the campsite or overnight fees. Apps like All Stays, Compendium, Ultimate Campground or FreeCampsites.net can come in handy.

- **Make Full Use of Your Memberships** – Time to cash in on those RV memberships to help you cut down the cost. One of the biggest perks of these memberships will be the discounts you can score on campground fees.

- **Longer Stays** – Staying in one spot longer is one way of saving money. A lot of campsites offer monthly, even weekly rates, which are much cheaper compared to paying for just one night. If you find a spot you like, consider staying put a little longer. Not moving around as much saves on the gas bill too.

- **Shopping for Fuel** – An RV is a gas guzzler, and you'd be surprised at how much you're going to end up spending to fill up your tank. Even the smallest RVs are still going to guzzle a lot more gas than what your car would have. Apps like GasBuddy are going to help you check out which gas stations are currently offering the most affordable fuel prices, and in this case, it definitely pays to drive a few extra miles if it means you save more money in the long run.

- **Picking the Right Places** – Some cities cost more than others to stay in. New York is going to cost you more to stay in than somewhere like Alabama for example. That doesn't mean you should skip out on expensive destinations, but being flexible and taking in all the potential costs involved, will help you better prepare for it financially. If you know where you're (or want to go) is going to cost slightly more, work a couple of extra jobs to help fund the cost. Find out the campground fees, the cost of local groceries and recreational activities. It's all about financial and logistical planning.

- **Shoulder Season Is Your Friend –** Some spots can be pretty pricey during peak season, even places like National Parks. To save some dollars, shoulder season is now going to be your best friend. Shoulder season is simply visiting tourists spots during their off-peak periods or whenever their visitor number rates are on the low end. With smaller crowds and lower prices, you still get to do the activities that you wanted, without the hefty price tag that goes along with it.

- **Do Your Own Cooking –** Your RV already comes with a built-in kitchen, so you might as well put it to good use.

Cooking at home is always going to be more cost-effective than eating out, even at cheap restaurants. Consider making your meals from scratch, it saves big bucks at the end of the day.

- **Planning Ahead** – Being spontaneous and living in the moment is one of the best things about RV living. Still, if you're thinking about your finances, the smartest thing to do is going to be to plan ahead as much as possible, even with last minute plans. Last minute accommodation, not enough groceries or gas in the tank to make the trip can translate into some pretty expensive last minute scrambling.

- **Be Your Own Handyman** – You're going to be on the go most of the time, and getting used to being your own handyman is something you're going to have to get used to. Professional repairs can get expensive, especially around the holidays. Developing some basic skills for minor repairs means you don't have to fork out cash each time there's a little repair that needs to be made.

- **Boondocking** – Campsite fees are definitely cheaper than what it would cost for you to stay in a hotel, but without a steady paycheck, even the little sums can add up to pretty big amounts quicker than you realize. For a more affordable option that isn't going to cost you an arm and a leg, give boondocking a try. Boondocking, sometimes referred to as dry camping or dispersed camping, is simply camping out on public lands without any of the little luxuries that come with a regular campsite. Sure, you might have to learn how to maximize and conserve your water and power, but the minimal fees are much lower, and if you're lucky, some places might even let you camp out there for free.

Getting Ready to Live In An RV Full-Time

As you get ready to begin your journey as a full-time nomad enjoying all the freedom that life has to offer, you're going to need a couple of checklists to ensure that you're well and truly prepared for what's ahead of you.

Let's start with your personal supplies checklist. The last thing you want is to be halfway on your journey only to realize there's a couple of things you've completely forgotten about. Buying new items is going to cut into the budget you've set for yourself, so to avoid that, a checklist comes in handy. Here's what you're going to need:

- Personal belongings (clothes, mobile phone, laptop, phone and laptop chargers, camera, sunglasses, keys, medication if needed, video equipment, guidebooks and maps).

- Financial items (cash, credit card, checks, emergency fund).

- Personal documentation (insurance, drivers ID, RV registration documents, RV operating manuals).

- Essential contact numbers (tow vehicle, roadside assistance, emergency contact numbers).

- Sleeping equipment (pillows, extra pillows, blankets, bedsheets, bedspreads, mattress protector, pajamas).

- Kitchen equipment (utensils, toaster, coffee machine, coffee pot, dishes, can opener, containers, corkscrew, cutting board, knives, tongs, zip lock bags, Tupperware, napkins, picnic blanket, tablecloth, cleaning supplies).

- Tools (duct tape, hammer, wrench, screwdrivers, flashlight, pliers, sockets, wheel wrench, motor oil, emergency tires, batteries, jumper cables, tire pressure gauge, cutters, wire connectors, coolant and jack).

- Miscellaneous supplies (tarp, extra tables and chairs, BBQ set, paper, pens, pencils, extension cords, adaptors and bungee cords).
- Pet supplies (litter box, doggy bags, food and water containers, food supplies, leash, collar, pet toys ID tags, health certification).

That is a rough guide as to what your personal items checklist would look like. Again, the items on it could be very different, depending on your needs.

Now, let's say you've decided not to sell your home after all because you still want to return home someday after fulfilling all your wanderlust bucket list items. In that case, you're going to need a checklist to make sure all your affairs are in order since you're going to be gone for a long time. Before you head out, check that:

- Your lights and fans are turned off, including air conditioner or heater.
- All the windows are securely locked.
- All the doors have been securely locked
- The garage door is locked.
- All the closets, kitchen cabinets and drawers have been shut.
- All the trash has been emptied out.
- The house is nice and clean before you leave.
- All electronic items have been unplugged.
- All the main water faucets have been turned off.
- Your neighbors and family who will be dropping in and checking on the house have your contact details and know how to reach you.

Recommended Equipment Needed

There's a lot more that goes into owning an RV than you might have initially realized. That's because you're not just buying an RV, you're buying a combination of a vehicle and a home. Double duty means more responsibilities, and every RV must have all the recommended equipment that comes with owning such a vehicle so your journey is as safe and comfortable as possible.

The list of recommended equipment for RV ownership includes:

- A drinking hose for your freshwater tank
- Surge protectors and EMS (30 and 50 amp)
- An adapter: for example, if you have a 30-amp plug, you may need an adapter to step down to 15 amps at most RV parks as well as for hooking up to other equipment, like a 15 amp plug generator. A surge protector is also highly recommended to protect your rig and electrical equipment. Some RV parks have bad power hookups, so you want to protect yourself and your RV

- Generator
- Air compressor: an air compressor is really good to have on the road to maintain the air pressure in your tires as needed. You don't want to slack off on taking care of your tires. Low tire pressure equals blown tires, sometimes at the worst times imaginable!
- A torque wrench to check your RV's lug nut torque. It's recommended that you perform this check before taking off each and every trip. Be sure also that you have an appropriately sized socket to fit your RV lug nuts. A tire pressure gauge is another essential for checking tire pressures every time you leave a site.
- GPS
- Showerhead
- Water pressure regulator
- Water filter
- Laundry bag
- Hammock
- Propane fire pit

- Grill and grilling utensils
- Sewer hose and connector
- Sewer hose support
- Leveling blocks
- Disposable gloves
- Laptop stand
- Hotspot antenna
- Solar batteries
- Lithium batteries
- Roof gutter drip extenders
- Dicor sealant and caulk gun is a great thing to have on hand, especially if you have a rubber roof. You'll want to inspect the roof regularly to check for cracks.
- Walkie-talkies (if you're not traveling alone)

Last recommendation: Tires. A common sentiment among the RV community is that the tires you get from the factory on a brand-new trailer are not great quality, and you will need to plan to invest in some good tires that are graded for above the weight they are going to be carrying.

This is an advice I hear a lot from full-time RV-ers. Buy tires that are designed to handle even more weight than your trailer's weight to make sure they are going to handle your RV when it's loaded with everything you're going to be towing. Check the pressures often, as well as that lug nut torque. And remember, an essential to have on the road is wheel chocks and levelers. These stabilize the RV when you're parked, making sure your rig is securely in place and doesn't move around.

You might consider getting tire covers to protect your tires from the sun, as letting your tires bake in the sun for extended periods of time will wear them prematurely and cause them to degrade much more quickly than they would if protected.

Never be in a hurry on the road. Take your time getting from point A to point B and don't push it with your RV. You'll regret it, and it can be quite dangerous while towing a heavy rig. Also, remember that all that weight is going to take much longer to stop than what you are used to in your normal vehicles.

Legal Residence, Domicile, Banking, and Health Insurance

With your RV equipment and supplies sorted out, the next considerations to think about would be the legality considerations of living in an RV. Different state laws and statues are something you're going to encounter on the road if you're planning to do it full time. Insurance is going to be of the utmost importance, and like every other vehicle, your RV must be insured against any potential accidents which may take place. All your documentation should be up to date before you head out on your journey.

Leasing the Land

A quick check on the local state laws where you're currently based will tell you what the basic requirements are to own an RV, which will help you determine the kind of insurance coverage you'll need. If you're unsure and think that some professional assistance might help you make a better decision, consider engaging the services of a lawyer whose specialization includes RV accidents and injuries.

Then there are legal considerations of land leasing to consider. Since RVs are huge and take up a lot of space, you're not going to be able to just park your vehicle at any available parking spot like you would with a car. To park your RV, the land needs to be leased, and it is important to make the necessary booking and preparations before your arrival to minimize the complications or problems which might arise.

When you lease the land to park your RV in, you become a tenant. Some RV owners who have committed to living in their little camper full time might find that purchasing a piece of land to be the easier option so they don't have to deal with the hassle of lease agreements. However, if you're on the move from one location to another frequently, then leasing is one of your options. Considering you are a tenant in this case, as with renting any piece of property, it is important to familiarize yourself with your tenant's rights to avoid any legal complications or issues with your landlord. Always be sure to sign a written agreement and have it in writing to protect yourself.

Getting to Know the State Laws

Every state has their own set of laws to abide by, and to save yourself from incurring a possible fine or ticket, before your arrival get to know the local state laws of where you're headed. Some of the aspects which might differ according to state include warranties, roadside assistance programs. Some states are also more RV friendly than others.

Domicile and What It Means

Are you familiar with the legal term *domicile?* Most first-time Rvers would only begin to come across the term when they're getting ready to go on the road. Domicile is the term which is used to refer to the location that you intend to make your permanent place to call home. This is going to be the place you plan on coming back to after a temporary absence. This permanent home of yours will – the state where you live in, so to speak – is going to be where you pay your taxes, register your vehicle, get your driver's license and health insurance and handle all your banking needs.

Domicile is not going to be the same as a residence. You are allowed to have multiple residences at any given time, but you are only allowed to have *one domicile*. When thinking about changing the state of your domicile, you're going to need to provide proof of intent. This means that if you acquire a new mailing address but still keep all your driver's license, voting registration rights and bank accounts from your old state, it is going to be tough to prove your intention to switch locations. Establishing a domicile state requires that you cut ties with your former state before you can commit to the new one.

As an Rver, the easiest option for you would probably be to just maintain your domicile in the current state that you live, since all your official and legal documentation, paperwork and banking has already been conducted there for some time anyway. Your driver's license and RV registration would most likely have been done in your home state too. A lot of Rvers prefer to just stick to the original state they currently have, since it's far less hassle.

However, you might want to consider that this might not be an option you want to stick with forever. When you're on the move a lot, things change all the time, and having to return all the back to your home state for official matters like license renewal or vehicle inspection when you're already on the other side of the country might become a hassle. Plus, if your state's tax burdens are higher compared to a lot of other places, it might not make financial sense for you to keep paying high taxes in a place that you don't technically live full-time anymore. If this is going to be a factor that you want to consider, shopping around for a better, more strategically located domicile state might make more sense, depending on your situation.

When choosing a state as your domicile, there are going to be several factors you want to consider, which include:

- The ease of establishing a domicile in the state.
- Mail-forwarding services available for use. If you know someone who's address

you can use, have a chat with them and see if that's a workable option.

- State taxes, income taxes, property taxes, and any other taxes.
- Ease of vehicle registration.
- Required state vehicle inspections where you may need to return to this state more often than you plan to (if applicable).
- Cost of licensing and registration.
- Auto insurance premium options.
- Health insurance options that meet your needs.
- Location of the state.
- Ease of voter registration.
- Home-schooling laws (if you have kids to consider).

If you do want to switch your domicile state, here are the steps that you need to start taking to get the process going:

- Get yourself a mailing address in the new state you want to be domiciled in. A mail-forwarding service would work just fine in this case.

- File for a change of address with your local post office.
- Get your health insurance from the new state.
- Get your auto insurance from the new state.
- Get any other insurance that you might need from the new state.
- Register your vehicle in the new state (you might have to travel to get this done).
- Get your driver's license done in the new state.
- Register yourself as a voter in the new state.
- De-register yourself as a voter in your old state.
- Establish as many professional and legal ties as possible with your new state.

The Best States for Rvers to Establish a Domicile

While everyone might have their own preference of a state to set up their domicile, there are some states which are more popular among Rvers than others, and these states are:

- Florida
- South Dakota
- Texas

These three fare better than others when it comes to an Rvers choice of a domicile because their low taxes, nomad lifestyle friendly policies and the mail-forwarding services which they provide.

South Dakota for example, makes it easy for nomad Rvers to get everything that they need easily, from the driver's license to vehicle registration. South Dakota has no state income or personal property tax, and only imposes a 4% excise tax on vehicle purchases. You'll be pleased to know that there are no state vehicle inspections either, so you're free to roam forever and only return when you feel like it. As a bonus, South Dakota also has among the lowest rates for auto insurance in the country. It may be a little out of the way for a lot of Rvers location wise, but the perks alone make the trip there worth it.

Another popular favorite amongst Rvers is Florida, with no state income tax and no taxes imposed on RVs being one of the biggest attractions which has nomads flocking to the East coast. Compared to either Texas of South Dakota, Florida has a much broader range of health insurance options for you to choose from. With no state vehicle inspection requirements, you're free to come and go whenever you like.

Texas is also a favorite amongst full-time Rvers. Like South Dakota, it has no state income tax or taxes imposed on vehicle transfers. In terms of voting and getting your hands on absentee ballots, everything can be done via mail for your convenience. Texas does require you to return for vehicle inspections, but they've made it easier on you by allowing you to defer if you can't return to the state immediately.

Banking on the Road

Thanks to the Internet, dealing with all your banking needs is easier than ever and can be done anywhere with a good internet connection. Internet banking is an Rvers best friend, since it makes managing and handling all your financial needs convenient, easy and accessible no matter where you are.

What you're going to frequent the most while you're on the road is the ATM Machines for the times when you need to use good old cold hard cash for certain transactions. To make things easier on yourself, consider choosing a national chain bank to save on fees when you access those ATM machines out of town. Bank of America is one option to consider, since every time you use an ATM machine which is not part of your local banking system, you will be charged a fee for the transaction.

Paying bills online is easy enough if you've got the banking apps on your phone and a good internet connection. Most companies these days let you make payments online through EFTs (electronic fund transfers), which makes things a lot easier. Even balancing your checkbook can be done on your bank's website.

Getting Your Health Insurance Done

Since most Rvers are going to be working for themselves, they'll need to purchase their health insurance through what's known as a marketplace. This means getting yourself enrolled through the Affordable Care Act. Your options for healthcare are going to depend on where your state of residency is. You'll also once to source for a plan that provides national coverage, so you're protected no matter where you are. Remember the three best states for domicile which were mentioned earlier? Well, usually the most popular domicile states *also* come with the best health insurance options.

Florida is one state which has some of the best healthcare benefits for those who are Rving full time. Some of their options are the cheapest and most comprehensive choice of health insurance around, and you can travel with peace of mind knowing that you're covered during your trip. Florida Blue, for example, is one of the more prominent insurers in the state, and the available options for full-time Rvers are more affordable than you think.

Food Prep and Storage on Your RV

Since living in a RV isn't going to be the same as living at home, you're probably wondering how it's going to affect your food prep and storage. An RV does come with its own kitchen, but it's going to be a lot smaller than the one you have at home, which means a lot of the recipes and food you prepare might suddenly become a challenge in such a confined space. Food storage too isn't going to be nearly as simple as living at home. While there may have been no shortage of cabinets and kitchen drawers at home, an RV has limited space and a smaller fridge to work with, which means food storage needs to be kept to a minimum due to a lack of room.

The best tip you could bring with you on the road for your food prep and storage is to keep things as simple as possible. Other tips to make things easier would be:

- Store your food containers away *before* you start driving. Your RV moves around a lot, and anything that is not weighted down is going to tip and spill over.
- Avoid storing your food in glass containers to minimize any broken glass mishaps from happening.
- Pack leftovers in baskets, Tupperwares, cartons, containers or zip lock bags for easy storage.

- Use lightweight tableware, containers and tumblers, since heavy drinking glasses and large heavy dishes are not practical for RV travel.
- Avoid bringing high-risk perishables with you on the road since your fridge could easily get warm during the day. Items with a longer shelf life and canned goods work best for RV travel.
- Picking smaller sized packets will save you storage space in your shelves and cupboards, which makes it more practical for an RV.

Sticking to a healthy meal plan when you're on the go on the time can be a challenge to maintain. All those restaurants you're going to pass along the way, not to mention the array of snacks at the gas stops will tempt you to go off course with your intention to eat healthy. Quick tips to help you stay as healthy as possible during your travels are to:

- Pick up healthier snack options instead when that craving hits. Trail mixes, nuts, seeds, dried fruit, fruits and vegetables are a much healthier option and you don't feel so guilty munching on these.
- Shop at farmers markets for healthier food choices. These goods are usually modestly priced, and the ingredients are fresher than what you might get at the supermarket.
- Create a weekly menu that you stick to instead of deciding on the spur of the moment. This makes it much easier to stick to a healthy meal plan when you meal prep in advance.
- Keep recipes short and simple, and pick a couple of menus that you rotate through so you don't get bored of the same thing.

Chapter 3: Let's Do It! Buying the Perfect RV

Alright, now that you've decided to heed the call of the nomadic lifestyle, you're all set and ready to get the ball rolling. Once you've sorted out your finances, made preparations to begin selling your home, choosing a domicile state and handling the rest of the paperwork that needs to be done, here comes the next big question. *What kind of RV should you choose?*

Motorhomes, Trailers and Campers

Have you started shopping around for your RV? If you have, you've probably realized by now that there's a lot of options to choose from. Picking the perfect one suddenly doesn't seem so easy when there's a lot to think about before deciding. You're about to spend quite a hefty sum of money, and you want to be sure you're completely satisfied with your choice of RV.

Choosing your very first RV is going to be like choosing a home. Technically, an RV is a home of sorts, except that it comes with wheels instead of being rooted to the ground. Just like what it was selecting your first home, your choice of RV is going to be based on your needs, budget and lifestyle that you want to go with to help you narrow down your selection criteria.

There are a couple of questions that need to be addressed before choosing your RV, which include:

- Are you looking for a camper van version of an RV or a big rig?
- Do you want to drive a Class A, Class B or Class C type of RV?
- Are there any fees which are not included in the current ticket price?
- What's the cost of registering the RV you have in mind?
- If you're going with a financing option, what are the details of the policy?

If you're buying a second-hand RV, then your questions are also going to include:

- How many owners has this RV seen before?
- What is the RV's history?
- Are there any maintenance records that come with it?
- Is this under warranty?
- Does the purchase come with a service package included?

- Does the person who is responsible for showing you the RV the owner too?
- When were the tires last replaced and how many miles have they clocked?

Sifting through all the available options, weighing the pros and cons could take you weeks, maybe even months to decide. Researching online forums, reading up on articles and other various consumer reports and reviews, wading through all that information is not a process which should be rushed. This is a big commitment you're making, and it's not technically cheap either. You want to be sure you're making it worth your while and every dollar spent count for something.

To make things a little easier for you first-time RV buyers especially, these are the considerations you want to bear in mind to help you decide on your RV:

- **Think About Your Camping Style -**
  Do you intend to do this full-time, or just
  for a couple of months on and off during
  your vacation periods. For full-timer
  RVers, a bigger RV might make more
  sense since this is literally going to be
  your permanent home.

- **Going Solo? -** The RV size you decide
  on is going to be determined by whether
  you're going on this adventure alone or
  with company. More people means
  bigger RVs are needed of course, and
  even those can feel pretty cramped
  sometimes when you're all confined in a
  space together.

- **Do You Intend to Do a Lot of
  Travelling? -** Again, would depend on
  whether you're doing this long or short
  term. You should also consider whether
  you plan to actively move around a lot,
  never staying in one place for too long, or

if you plan to settle in one location for a period of time before heading off again to your next destination. Bigger RVs and frequent travel mean more fuel consumption.

- **Living Area** - If you've got a logistics plan already going, this is going to help you out here. The places you intend to park at each destination should be a factor for consideration when selecting your RV type. Keep in mind and not all states are RV-friendly, and some public spaces like state parks are usually not able to accommodate anything bigger than a 32-foot and below RV. In areas where public spaces are limited, smaller camper vans work best since they're much easier to park. Larger RVs like the Class A motorhomes work best in campsites with full amenities.

The Best Places to Get an RV

Whenever there's an RV show in town or dealers are having a sale, attend them. RV shows are great during your research phase, since you get to examine for yourself all the different options available and ask the salespeople as many questions as you'd like. It's a great way to observe the different styles, choices and type of RV built all in the convenience of one location.

Consider frequenting several RV shows prior to settling on a model to give you a better perspective. You want to be sure you're making an informed decision and not rushing into the process. Visit as many RV dealerships as you can too and take a look at all the available models. Ask if you could test drive a couple to get the feel of what it would be like. Salespeople will be a good source of info, and they might even share some helpful tips of their own.

Time to Choose Your RV

This is going to be *very different* from driving a car. It's more than just picking up your keys, sticking them in the ignition and hitting the gas pedal to go. Owning, maintaining and even driving an RV is going to be a completely new experience, and for first-timers, there's going to be a lot to take in.

Let's get started with the type of RVs available for purchase:

- **Class A Motorhomes** - If you're looking for an all-in-one with every amenity you could possibly need, the Class A motorhome would be perfect for you. Ideal for long distance travel, this model is the most suitable option to go for when you travel with a family in tow. With all the bells and whistles included, be prepared to fork out anywhere from $60,000 and upwards for a new model.

- **Class B Motorhomes** - These models have got similar amenities like the Class A version, except that they smaller and similar to what it would feel like to drive around a large SUV. If you're only travelling with one other person, Class B might make a lot more sense compared to the Class A option. The price range is *slightly* cheaper, ranging from $40,000 to $80,000 for a new model.

- **Class C Motorhomes** - Class C is a combination of both the Class A and B versions. If you're only looking to rent an RV for the summer or short-term stays, the Class C is among the more popular options, since it's much easier to maneuver compared to the other two classes, and still enough for a family to be comfortable in short-term. Depending on the size, the price tag for these variants start at $50,000 and upwards for the new models.

- **Travel Trailers -** The advantage that these variants have is that their lightweight, yet sturdy at the same time, which makes them much easier to tow compared to the heavier Class models. Since these models can easily be towed by your average pickup truck, minivan or SUVs, you could save yourself some money and in a case of emergency, anyone with a truck, SUV or minivan nearby will be able to help you out. A new model could set you back anywhere from $15,000 to $30,000 on average, depending on the trailer's size, material, layout and amenities which are included.

- **Fifth Wheel -** If you're wondering why they're named fifth wheels, it's because they can easily be attached to a bigger trailer using a hitch pin. Ranging anywhere from 18 to 40 feet long, fifth wheelers are much easier to park compared to a conventional trailer, and the average price tag on a new model is approximately $35,000.

- **Pop-up Camper -** If you're on the lookout for the most economical model that you could own, pop-up trailers are the way to go. Being the smallest and lightest out of all the trailer options, a new version of these starts at $8,000 and can go all the way up to $20,000. The pop-up though is nothing more than just a tent with wheels, so it's not the most viable option for full-time RV living on its own.

- **Truck Bed Campers -** Mobile travelling doesn't get any better than a truck bed camper. You'd be surprised at how much space these truck bed campers come with, and some models even have the option of extending the legs right down to the ground. If you already own a decent sized pickup truck, don't plan on RVing full-time and you don't fancy the idea of towing a big trailer behind you, truck bed campers are perfect for those short term vacations. Expect to start at a price tag of $3,000 for the lower end models, but they can range to an upwards of $40,000.

What About a Van Instead?

The decision of whether to go with a van or an RV is going to be an entirely personal choice. When comparing any model against each other, you're going to want to look at the pros and cons of course. If you choose to go with an RV, the pros that you can look forward to include:

- Having a bathroom on-board.
- Plenty of seating room (depending on the size of your RV, but it's usually enough to accommodate you and any guests you may have).
- A spacious refrigerator by RV standards

- Ample sleeping space
- Being able to plug into power when you arrive at RV sites.

The downsides you can expect if you go with the RV option are:

- Poor gas mileage.
- Storage space may not be as efficient as you'd like (depending on the size of your RV).
- The constant need to buy propane to keep your refrigerator going.
- A fee that must be paid at the RV sites, since plugging into power doesn't exactly come for free.
- The noisy generator which keeps running when you're not plugged in somewhere. Otherwise, your onboard appliances are not going to work without the generator.
- Dealing with your own sewage can be extremely disgusting to some people.

- You feel like you're driving around a tank.

Now, compare that to if you were to go with the van option instead, the pros that you can come to expect when you choose a van include:

- The gas mileage is a lot more decent compared to the bigger RVs.
- The interior can be customizable to your specific needs.
- Cozy enough, despite not being as spacious.
- Most vans these days would come with an external battery bank for you to charge what you need.
- It is much easier to park and drive these things compared to an RV.

The downside to going with the van option would be the:

- Limited space for sleeping and seating.

- Not as sturdily built compared to the RV.
- Limited space means a lot of storage considerations may need to be compromised.
- No onboard bathroom, which means having to go into nature to do your business.

Some factors which are going to play a role in your decision are:

- **Your Budget -** Yes, it all comes down to the numbers again. What you're willing to spend on realistically vs what you would like to have if you could. Given that a steady job is most likely not in a picture anymore, budgeting becomes a factor in almost every decision that gets made from here on out, including the type of motorhome you end up going with. If you're not particular about driving only brand new models, the older versions of the Class A and Class C RVs come with a more manageable price tag. You could easily score a decent model for under $10,000, but it might be a fixer-upper that needs some work done.

- **Gas Mileage -** Bigger rigs are of course going to come with less than desirable gas mileage. If this is not a big factor for you, and you're planning to spend at least 3 months or more relaxing and camping out at one location before moving onto the next, bigger RVs are of course going to be significantly more comfortable than the van variety. Don't forget to factor in your monthly budget too, and what you can realistically afford to spend on gas without breaking the bank.

- **Where You Plan to Be -** Picture this for a moment. When you see yourself already immersed in the RV life, where do you picture yourself spending most of your parked days? In campgrounds or RV parks? A forest or somewhere close to the beach? Perhaps you don't see yourself stopping anywhere for too long because the wanderlust spirit in you makes you want to keep moving from one destination to the next. Where you plan on spending most of your parked days is going to help you decide whether an RV or van is going to make the most sense. In RV campgrounds and parks, vehicles which are 30 feet and under can be accommodated at just about any park or site. Some parks may be able to make some room for the larger variants. Smaller vans make it easier to park just about anywhere, even if it's not a designated campsite, which makes them the better option for overnight sleeping. You could easily get away with overnight sleeping in cities or towns using a smaller van, which might not be so easy to do if you've got a bigger RV on your hands.

- **Is Comfort a Must? -** If you're doing to be doing this full-time, then probably yes, comfort should be a factor in this equation. You want to be comfortable in your own home, and if comfort is a priority, then RVs with the full range of amenities is the clear choice for you. If you don't plan to spend a lot of time inside your RV when you're parked out, then comfort might not be quite as high on your list of priorities, and you'd be happy to make do with smaller vans that still come with the basic amenities needed for comfortable living.

That being said, it is going to be hard to guess with 100% certainty what you're going to need to be comfortable out there, and what you'd be happy to do without until you've actually tested these models out for yourself. Some RVs who have been doing this for a long time have gone through several models, from big RVs to the smaller van variety, depending on their needs and requirements at the time. And of course, if they had the budget to do so. This may be your home, but it doesn't have to be your *permanent* home if you feel like you need a change of model.

Buying a Used RV - What You Need to Know

Let's say that buying a second-hand RV is going to be better suited to your budget and you've decided to go down that route, what do you need to know before finalizing your purchase? Let's take a look at the list:

- Check the RV for any possible dents or scratches and ask about what happened to cause those dents.
- Check the RV for any stains on the walls, corners and floors.
- Check the RV for possible leaks around the windows or vents.

- Are all the fans and lights in working order? What about all the onboard appliances?
- Do any of the door hinges need replacing?
- Check your side mirrors and ensure they've provided you with good visibility.
- Check that you're able to start the RVs engine on the first try without any problems.
- Listen out for any unusual noises which may come up once you've got the engine running for some time.
- Check that the RVs brakes and in good working condition.
- Once you've got the engine running a fair bit, go around the back and see what kind of smoke the RV emits.
- Play around with the RVs controls to test that everything is working as it should.
- Check that the RVs steering wheel is in good shape.
- Do the tires need replacing?

- Turn on all the taps, faucets, water heater and tanks to make sure they're all working and there are no leaks anywhere. Also, a good time to check that the water pressure is okay.
- Check the RVs holding tanks for any possible leaks.
- Check the carpets if there are any that are included in the RV.
- How are the seats looking like? Are they still comfortable? Still good with no holes ripped in them?
- What about sleeping spaces? Are they still in good condition?
- Be sure your RV has no rust spots on any of its exterior compartments.
- Does the RV still come with its original manuals and full maintenance records?
- How's the condition of the house batteries?

Always be sure to take your RV out for a test run, more than once if the owner is willing to comply.

You're going to need to double check that everything is running smoothly before you commit to making the purchase. That's a long list to go through, but it's better to be thorough with any major purchase you're making. It's always best to deal with directly with the previous owner of the RV so you can ask as many questions as possible.

Finding Low-Cost RVs and Negotiating Your Best Price

Getting a good deal on anything is always a good thing. If it means the chance to save you a couple hundred bucks, why not? Brush up on your negotiation skills, because you're going to need them to help you land the best price for your RV.

If you're going this full-time, an RV is going to be a very important investment. Finding low-cost RVs and getting a good price for them should be one of your top priorities in a bid to save some money which could then be redirected towards better use.

To start scouring for RVs at a bargain and negotiate the best deal for your purchase, here's what you need to do:

- **Leaving Your Options Open** - Keep an open mind when it comes to shopping around for good RV deals. Taking your time and looking at as many prices as possible will allow you to better compare which option is going to be more value for money.

- **Head to RV Shows** - Most dealers would be eager to offer you a great deal at RV shows if only to avoid the cost of towing and sending the RV back if it doesn't sell. Plus, since they work on commission, you'll have a better chance of negotiating a good deal if the dealers are eager to sell.

- **End of Season Purchases -** Buying an RV is similar to buying a car at an auto dealership. RV dealers too have a monthly or annual target that they need to meet. If they haven't met their quota just yet by the time the end of the season is approaching, they'll be keen to sell as many as possible to hit their mark. This is when you waltz in and try to negotiate yourself a bargain.

- **Wait For A Sale -** Sales do take place every now and again. Special promotions, price slashes, major discounts on prices are offered by RV dealers every now and then. Why not wait for a sale before you make a purchase? You'd definitely be getting a better deal than if you were to buy during off-sale periods.

- **Be Willing to Take Risks -** You have to be willing to be risky with your negotiations. Don't be afraid to start with a reasonably low offer and start negotiating your way up from there until you and dealer can come to a price you agree on. If they disagree immediately with your starting bid, don't be afraid to walk away. There'll always be other dealers and other bargains.

- **Let Go Of the "Brand" Mentality -** By limiting yourself to only wanting to purchase a particular brand, you're limiting your options of getting the best possible deal. Sure, you may have a preference, but if saving money is your priority, you need to unchain yourself from being loyal to just one brand and be open to shopping around.

Driving Tips for Beginners

Ready to take your RV on the road? It's normal for first-timers to experience some nervousness. It's not hard to see why this aspect is one of the scariest when it comes to thinking about embarking on a full-time RV journey. Depending on the size of your RV, you've probably never driven anything that big in your life.

There's no way to sugar coat it: It's gonna be scary the first time you get behind the wheel of an RV.

Hopefully, you've rented an RV or perhaps taken one for a test-drive and your first time in front of an RV you own is not the very first time period. Anyway, whatever the case, there really is no way around the fact that you are going to have to practice and learn entirely new strategies for driving something like an RV.

But don't get discouraged, and don't let a few nerves get in the way of what you want if you are passionate about living a mobile life. We tend to scare ourselves out of trying things sometimes as human beings, and this is a great way to miss out on the best experiences of your life.

Depending on the type of RV you're driving there will be some different things to think about. Remember, too, that there are courses out there that are available, online and in person, that can help you orient yourself as you start practicing for the first time.

Obviously, adjusting your mirrors to their appropriate positions is a vital first step. Be sure to be sitting straight up in the driver's seat while you're doing this. Don't be leaning forward or to the side. You want to be able to easily glance over and see what you need to see without having to adjust your position too much.

Many instructors suggest making use of markers on your mirror, for example, to point out the pivot point for where your motorhome begins to pivot on a turn. There are lots of videos on YouTube available with seasoned drivers to guide you through how to do this, but the idea is to give yourself as much of an advantage as possible for determining where the tail end of your RV is going to go in order to take as much guesswork out of the process as possible. Having a visual marker is a big advantage here. As always, go slowly and take your time, especially at the beginning. There's no sense in rushing and wrecking your brand-new $50,000 RV!

Backing up is probably the scariest aspect of driving an RV for newbies. I've known lots of people who don't feel comfortable parallel parking their tiny sedans, let alone a 30-foot trailer.

One of the important things to nail down in this scenario is knowing intimately how much your back end swings out as you turn, or "tail swing." This swing will be determined by how long your RV extends behind the rear axle.

One of the best things you can do is take the RV out to an empty parking lot or deserted area, and just practice moving the RV around. Use cones to help guide you as you maneuver in different directions, and while backing up. One rule of thumb is that there will be about 1 foot of swing for every 3 feet the trailer extends behind the rear axle. Line up your RV's wheels with a painted pine or another marker, then try making a sharp turn. Observe the tail swing that is created after driving in that turn a few feet. You can quickly see how important it is to be aware of this swing in order to avoid hitting something on the street or near the street on the sidewalk or grass. Something that doesn't look like it's in the way may suddenly turn in to a problem if you've underestimated the tail swing on your trailer. Imagine pulling up to fill up with gas or diesel, then when you pull out, underestimating how much that tail end is going to move once you turn out. This will start to come naturally once you practice driving, just as with any skill.

If you have the opportunity and the space, set up a little course for yourself with cones or other markers to practice backing up and other maneuvers. When it comes to backing up, you'll want to start with practicing what is called straight line backing, which is exactly what it sounds like. You'll want to get comfortable and confident with backing up your trailer or motorhome in a straight line. Obviously, a trailer is going to behave differently from a motorhome, but backing up in a straight line is a pretty essential skill to have no matter what type of RV you have.

To do this properly, once you have your mirrors in the proper position, back up slowly, keeping your eyes on both mirrors. As you move backward, notice anytime the trailer starts to sway right or left. When this happens, turn the steering into the problem, so if the trailer starts to sway to the left, turn the wheel slowly to the left until the problem is corrected. When the trailer is realigned, return the steering wheel to a neutral position. Keep this up as you watch both mirrors. The more you practice, the longer you will feel comfortable maintaining this maneuver. You only need small movements to correct the swaying, no more than a half turn, usually only a quarter, but make sure you're moving slowly until you build confidence in your skills. Once you've mastered this skill, you're ready to tackle more challenging maneuvers. Remember, practice makes perfect!

Here is a little recap to help you get the best out of your driving experience and stay safe while you're on the move:

- **Remember: Go Slow On the Turns!** - Slow and steady will get you and your wide, long RV around the turns as safely as possible and keep you from hitting the curb. Go slow and take your time.

- **Brake Awareness** - Your RV is significantly heavier than your car was, and braking this thing is going to take slightly longer before your RV eventually slows down. Always maintain a safe distance from the vehicle in front to give yourself enough braking room to work with.

- **Parking Assistance** - Parking your RV, as told, can be a challenge, and if you're having trouble navigating it on your own, don't be shy about asking for help.

- **Watch Your Lane** - Check your side mirrors often to make sure you're not veering off into someone else's lane. Your RV is huge and it can be tricky to gauge if you're staying in your lane or not for first-time drivers. You'll get used to it eventually.

- **Plan Ahead for Bridges** - Always plan ahead and navigate your journey using GPS to avoid being caught near bridges where you're not going to be able to clear.

- **Low Gears for Hills -** Use low gears for hilly terrains like mountains when you go both uphill and even more so when you're downhill so you'll be able to control your speed.
- **Go for Training -** There are some excellent RV driver training schools to consider enrolling in to give yourself more confidence in handling your RV on the road.

The Best Tips to Make Your Life On the Road Comfortable and Easier

What a lot of first time RVers tend to miss most when they first hit the road is the creature comforts of home they were so used to. It's a luxury we often don't appreciate enough until we're left without it. Your RV may be smaller than the home you've grown accustomed to, but there are some things you could do to make your life comfortable and easier:

- **RV locks -** One of the things that most people would agree makes people feel comfortable is security. You want to feel safe and secure, both while you're in your RV and when you are out and about in a towing vehicle while your trailer is parked at your site. You can purchase RV locks on Amazon which you can affix to your RV. It uses a four-digit code to unlock. Continuing along the lines of RV security, a lot of people install a low-cost carbon monoxide alarm inside their RV, adding another layer of comfort and security while you are asleep or out.

- **Use Double Hooks -** Easily purchased from any home improvement store, these are great for hanging and organizing your clothes.

- **Use Towel Grommets -** These will come in handy to keep your towels organized neatly and off the floor. They can easily be purchased from the hardware store.

- **Use Shoe Pockets** - Shoe pockets are great for organizing not just your shoes, but for other items like your toiletries or makeup for example. They can easily be customized to fit your bathroom wall or door by trimming them down to size.

- **Invest In a Good Mattress** - Another upgrade you will want to consider is the bed in your RV. If you've got a nice big RV that comes with a queen or king size mattress, you might want to save a little money in the budget to possibly invest in a new comfortable mattress that fits in your RV. If you're going to be living in this thing full-time, having a comfortable place to sleep is an absolute must. If you don't want to invest in a brand-new thousand-dollar mattress, there are other things you can do. Buy a foam Serta pad or another topper to put on top of the mattress that came with the RV.

- **Invest In A Sleep Mask or Blackout Curtains** - Light can still seep through into your RV, even with the curtains drawn. If this affects your ability to fall asleep, consider investing in a sleep mask or blackout curtains to create a cozy environment.

- **Level Your RV** - Make use of your RV's stabilizers and levellers to keep it from moving around every time someone wakes up in the middle of the night (if you're not travelling alone that is).

- **Heated Water Supply Hose** - If you plan to camp in the wintertime in a place where it is actually going to feel a bit like winter (to each his own!), then you will be facing a whole different set of challenges from those you face in the summer in 90-degree heat. One constant threat is the risk of freezing water lines, so be sure to invest in a heated water supply hose to protect your water supply and hoses in the cold weather. Be sure to also utilize that water pressure regulator we talked about earlier.

On the inside of the RV, you will also want to do what you can to keep yourself as warm as possible during those cold months. Many RV-ers supplement the furnace heat with small space heaters. This may also help you save on propane usage. You can buy good quality heaters that are small as well as good quality, which saves you space. Be sure that your RV is well insulated to maintain heat inside the RV. Check the vents and secure your RV against the cold in order to avoid discomfort inside. Avoid letting too much humidity into the RV by opening a vent a bit while you're taking a hot shower and limiting meals that will require cooking that will release additional humidity into the air.

- **Ear Plugs -** Does even the slightest noise rouse you because you're a light sleeper? Earplugs might make for a more comfortable night's sleep uninterrupted.

There are several things you can do to stay as cool as possible, and these tips apply in a big way to those of you who will be boondocking. One of the easiest tricks to keep in mind is to remember to point the nose of your RV to the west when you park. As the sun goes down, you'll get a nice swath of shade on the awning side of your RV, creating a nice place to relax later in the day without the sun blazing in your face.

Keep your windows open at night if you like things cooler, and then in the morning while it is still cool, open up the windows and use fans to suck in that nice cool air before it starts to heat up. This will help you stay ahead of the heat and prepare the inside of your RV for the heat that is coming.

Use Reflectix to redirect the heat away from the surface of your RV. Cover the front windows and as many other window surfaces as you can. If you're in an RV where the cab is openly connected to the rest of the RV, invest in some blackout curtains and hang that between the cab and the rest of your RV and you will feel a noticeable difference in temperature. This is a good strategy for temperature control in either really hot or really cold weather.

The next tip for keeping things cool inside the RV is to do your cooking outside! You can buy reusable ice cubes called White Ice to keep in your freezer and use to keep your drinks cold all summer long without wasting water.

Checklist for Setting Up at Your Campsite

So you've found the perfect campsite, and you're excited to get parked and set up. It's important to set up correctly and learn to do it efficiently so that each time you set up camp, it's not a huge headache. Your setup process will be specific to your RV situation, of course. But we're going to outline a step-by-step guide to setting up an RV to give you an idea of what the process entails. Let's get started!

- **Park the RV -** First thing's first. If you're traveling with a partner or family, you'll ideally want to have someone outside the vehicle to help spot you while you park the RV. You want the RV to be in a good position for hookup and leveling purposes. Doing this by yourself is tricky, so if you are traveling solo, you might just ask someone nearby, like one of your new temporary neighbors, if possible, to help you out. Odds are they will be more than happy to help. Be sure to start the backing up process by giving yourself lots and lots of room to maneuver; usually, more than you think you need. It might take a little work to find the right angle to back into your site. Remember, you are not in a hurry, so take your time! Also, you might want to be on the phone with your spotter if they are a partner or family member so that you're not yelling at the top of your lungs to communicate.

- **Wheel Chocks and Stabilizers -** Now, you'll remember we talked about wheel chocks and stabilizers in the recommended equipment section. Before you set these up, you'll want to check and make sure that you are the proper distance from the water and power. You don't want to set up the chocks just realize once you get those hoses out that you are too far away to connect. This will be easy to eyeball once you get used to it, but the first couple of tries might be tricky, so be sure you're getting close enough. Also, if you have an RV with slides, you're going to want to make sure that you have enough space for the fully extended slides. Third, you'll want to level left to right to make sure in a good position before chocking up.

Once these things are checked, it's time to chock the tires. There are several different types and styles of wheel chocks, so you'll need to do your own research and definitely talk to others who have the same RV type and learn what they prefer as well as the reasons for why. Everyone is going to have slightly differing opinions on what's best, so it will be up to you and your research and your discretion to choose and purchase the chocks you prefer.

Once the wheels are securely chocked, then it's time (if you have a trailer) to disconnect your tow vehicle. Be sure to lower the tongue jack before disconnecting the tow vehicle.

Now you can level the trailer front to back using a bubble level or other device. Next, you'll deploy the stabilizers. Use leveling blocks as necessary.

- **Connect to water and electrical -** Remember to use the surge protector and adapter we talked about in the recommended equipment list. Use the water pressure regulator at the water source when you hook up your water hose.

Once you've hooked up, you're ready to deploy the slides in your trailer, if applicable. Be sure to check and make sure that there are no obstructions to the slides, like open cabinet doors, etc., that could get caught and damaged as you deploy the slides.

- **Lastly,** get your gloves on and get ready to hook up the sewer hose—everyone's favorite step. Once you've hooked up your sewer hose, release the black tank first. The black tank holds sewage water, and your gray tank holds wastewater, from shower, sink, etc. Once that's done, release the gray water lever, and this will help rinse out the hose.

Bonus Tips - Maintaining Your RV

You've paid a lot of money for your RV, and you want to do everything you can to keep it running in top form. The better maintained your RV is, the better it will retain its value for when you want to sell it off later on. Take a look at the best tips below to help you keep your RV in excellent condition:

- Oil filters should be changed regularly, along with the oil.
- Get your RV generator serviced on time.
- Inspect your roof regularly.
- Have your brakes checked regularly by a mechanic whenever you can.
- Replace your fuel and air filters, along with any other filters which might need replacing.
- Biodegradable RV toilet paper is going to keep your sewer system in good condition as long as possible.
- Always check your tire pressures before heading out.
- RV batteries should be checked before each trip.

Conclusion

Thank for making it through to the end of this book, hope it was informative and able to provide you with all of the tools you need to achieve your goals whatever they may be.

You're all set with the basics that you need to hit the road as a full-time nomad. In the next series, we'll take a more in-depth look at how Rvers can make money online and on the road, brush up on your campfire knowledge and how to find the right campground, which RV clubs you should join, even more details about boondocking and what it's like to bring your pets on the road with you.

Now that you've got a guide to work with about sorting out the important areas prior to starting your RV life, you've got a pretty good idea about what you can expect in terms of what it's going to be like to be a permanent nomad. The RV life is unlike anything you've ever done. The sheer freedom of being able to go wherever you want, anytime you want, no restrictions, no boundaries, no strict schedules to adhere to makes RV living the perfect, simple, low-stress way of life that could be everything you have been searching for an more. So, who's ready for their adventure of a lifetime?

Finally, if you found this book useful in any way and now you want to be a real RVer, I've reached my goal! But, if you are not convinced yet, just remember...

There's got to be more to life than just living 9-5...

Why wait until the aches and pains have started to set in when you could make a life-changing decision to live in the moment right here, right now?

More and more young adults are starting to hit the wide-open road now instead of waiting for retirement to set in, and they're choosing to live life the RV way, embracing the sense of adventure and excitement that goes along with it. What a life it is, when you can go absolutely anywhere your heart desires at any time, and bring your entire home with you!

RV Travel:

Your Guide to a Full-Time Nomad Life / RV Retirement. Start Traveling, Camping and Boondocking as an RVer!

Michael Van Brown

For Beth, Thanks for your help.

Introduction

Do you want to live a life on the road? This the book is what you've been waiting for!

The following chapters will discuss everything you ever wanted know, and need to know, to begin your life on the road as a full-time RV-er. Now is the time to educate yourself on what it will be like to adopt this lifestyle. Many people tend to think that they have to be a certain age to or be in specific life circumstances for it to make sense to change one's life in this way. But these are archaic ideas! Years ago, people tended to think of RV living as only for the older, affluent populations of the country. You had to have lots of money stored up to sustain the lifestyle and buy a fancy RV. You had to be well past the heyday of your career and be "done" with it and ready for retirement before it made sense to sell your home and that car or that minivan you used for years to cart around the kids. All of these ideas of what it looks like to be an RV-er are about as accurate as a broken calculator.

When you venture out into the world and look at the scene at RV camps across the US, you will find all different kinds of RVs and all different kinds of RV-ers! With today's gig economy, many young adults are choosing to live a "minimalist" RV life while working online as freelance professionals. Adults at the peak of their careers choose to go on the road and take their online businesses with them. RVs now come in all kinds of shapes and sizes to suit each person's lifestyle choices. There are few restrictions to choosing this lifestyle, and, most often, it is people's own minds that are the biggest obstacle when it comes to making the decision.

I won't lie to you; it is quite a transition when you've lived your whole life in a nice home with lots of furniture and "stuff" all around you. You may have lived with a two-car garage and a garden and a patio with nice outdoor furniture.

But if you've picked up this book, perhaps it's because you've recognized the itch to see and experience something more. After all, the view from your patio has been the same for years. How amazing would it be if you could choose your environment and the view you wake up to as often as you want?

Get ready, because in this second book you're going to walk through what it means to be a full-time RV-er, working on the road, and the modern-day RV lifestyle. This book serves as a perfect introduction and guide for those who are either just discovering the possibility of this lifestyle and wanting to learn more, or ready to jump in head-first!

Chapter 1: RVpreneurs—Work for RVers

We touched on ways to make money on the road while living full-time in an RV, but in this chapter, we'll dig in a little deeper into the possibilities and give you a better idea of what different situations might look like through examples from real full-time RV-ers.

Making Money Online

First of all, in order to make money online, you will obviously need to secure internet access while on the road. There are a few different options here. A Verizon Jetpack can serve as your mobile Hotspot internet device. A lot of users prefer Verizon for the widest coverage around the US, and they will typically choose some kind of unlimited plan so that they don't have to worry about going over any data limits while working online. Depending on the type of work you're doing, you may be spending a lot of time downloading or uploading online, or you may just need the occasional email access to talk to clients while editing a book through Word. Whatever the case, do some research and decide on an internet setup that will be consistent and fit within your budget. Remember, your work online will be your source of income, so invest in a good laptop (some people even have desktops in their RVs) that is going to perform the way you need it to for a long time. Just like tires, this is not an area where you should skimp trying to save money! It will bite you in the long-term.

Another point to consider as far as the internet goes is that even though networks like Verizon have a pretty good coverage area, there are going to be areas where you might want to camp where you just won't have network access. For this reason, it is important to plan ahead for where you are going in conjunction with your work needs. You might stay somewhere with good access most of the time throughout the year, then when you're ready to unplug and take a break from work, go out to that national park site you've been wanting to see and take a week or month or whatever you can do and this will be your "vacation." To improve your overall luck with cell signal, you might consider investing in a cell booster and installing it to help in those areas where the signal may be hit and miss.

Before we get in to some online work options and examples, we need to talk a little bit about how to adjust and transition to this type of work, especially if you are coming from a corporate environment, or in-store sales environment, or basically any work environment that set a routine for you: Get up at 6:30 am, make a quick pot of coffee and pour some in your travel mug, eat a banana or grab something from McDonald's on the way in to work, clock in or sit down at your cubicle, work till lunchtime, go out and scarf down Subway for 30 minutes, get back to work, stare at the clock for the last 2 hours, then clock out or turn your computer off at 5 or 6 pm. If this sounds familiar to you, then you're in for a big surprise as you transition to a remote, online work situation, and it's important that you prepare yourself for some of the unique challenges that this change is going to present.

Now, I know you're probably pretty excited at the prospect. I've met a lot of people who felt such an overwhelming sense of relief when they finally get out of those dead-end jobs where they'd been unhappy or bored or overworked. Moving to a situation in which you have more control is an incredible thing, especially if you get to do it while traveling to places you've never seen before. Your scenery changes whenever you want it to, and instead of commuting home from work to plop in front of a TV for the rest of the evening, you have so much to explore outside your RV, just waiting for you to go out and explore. It is truly a beautiful thing, but it's important to remember that this lifestyle is not a full-time vacation. And working remotely online is not always easy. It is difficult in ways you may not even expect.

Now, there are different possibilities for your work situation. The type of work we talked about earlier was freelance work. But you might also be one of those people with awesome companies that have worked out a remote work situation for you. If that's you, congratulations! Not everyone is going to have that opportunity, and it's great that you will be able to continue with a company that (hopefully) you respect and enjoy enough to stay on. I'm sure your responsibilities are going to look a little different, but you are not diving into a whole new career and skillset, aside from computer skills, so that's wonderful.

Whether you're jumping into a new freelance career or working remotely with a company you are familiar with, or even getting into a new position remotely, you'll need to prepare yourself for the kind of discipline and responsibility it takes to work independently. It was easy to know what to do and when to do it when you have someone constantly telling you those things. You might think that it will be no problem to suddenly get to be your own boss or work on your own schedule, but this can be deceptively challenging.

In the beginning, you may not feel this as much as when you really get going and on the road because you are excited and motivated and feeling the pressure of making everything work, and this is normal. But you will soon find that you need a routine of your own to stick to consistently, and that's because it can be way too easy to get distracted by other things you want to do or your partner or your kids, and you may end up taking longer to do things that you thought you'd need. You might have done away with those alarm clocks, so you sleep in as long as you want, then crawl out of bed to your computer at a different time every day, enjoying the fact that you no longer have to get up agonizingly early for work. But if you're like most people, you will find that your productivity will be variable and often go down if you do not set up some kind of regular, daily routine for yourself. If you've got a project that's due in a few days, you may feel tempted to procrastinate and leave most of the work for that last day, when you may not have time to complete properly or feel stressed out as you work an insanely long day trying to get everything done. You don't want this new amazing, freeing lifestyle to suddenly feel stressful because you aren't handling your work time appropriately, so here are some tips for making sure you successfully transition to this remote work lifestyle.

First of all, you need to try and set a time for getting up each day and a time to be at your computer. I know, you love that you don't have to do that anymore, but the truth is, you really do in most cases. We as human beings are just way too prone to getting lazy and putting forth the least amount of effort for the biggest payoff possible, it's just in our nature. When you slack off on setting goals and routines, then your productivity is going to slack off, too. Get up at the same time each day and be at your computer at the same time every day that you are working. Then, depending on the work you have to do and when it is due, plan out your workdays, setting goals for each and every day that you are working. You will soon get a feel for how much you can complete comfortably in a day, and this is key for planning out and setting daily goals. If you think you will need a total of 30 hours to complete a project, then figure out when you need to start working on it and how many hours a day you need to work in order to get that job done on time. It's a good idea to give yourself a little wiggle room in case something unexpected comes up or something takes longer than you thought it would. I promise, if you talk yourself in to taking a few days off and pushing all that work into a couple of days, you will not enjoy those free days because you'll be stressing about how much work you're going to have to do. It is much better for your overall quality of life and sanity to set manageable, comfortably goals one step at a time toward your goal. You'll get a strong sense of satisfaction at the end of each workday without feeling the stress of the work piling up that you did not get done.

You will want to have a dedicated workspace in your RV, if possible. I know some of you might go with something smaller, but it will feel a lot more comfortable and natural if you can arrange your space so that you have a good area in which to work during those working hours. Many RV-ers use the dining area as an office while working, then convert it to the dining area in the evening hours when they're ready to have a meal. You don't want to be stuck with an uncomfortable chair and nothing but your lap to set your laptop on to work, because this isn't going to be comfortable for long periods of time while you're working. Get creative and do what you need to do to make your space feel like a comfortable and natural workspace. It will take some time to get used to it, no matter what your space looks like, but the basics are long-term comfort and ease of use on your laptop or computer. You may also need a little space for a notebook or calendar or something to keep track of your workload. Sometimes you might be at a campsite where there is a picnic table right outside and you can work there sometimes, but you will definitely want to have a home base inside the RV that feels stable.

Remember, this is now your RV, and you are free to change things up and replace things inside as you see fit, just as you would in a new home. It may not occur to new full-time RV-ers, but you can totally rip out that little dinette area and install a desk there if that's something you think will work for you. People have done it before, and they'll do it again! This is your home. Make it what you want.

So, what types of jobs do people do full-time on the road? Well, we could probably go through a hundred pages just listing the possibilities, but some of these jobs include: consulting (working for your previous employer as a consultant), blogging, online workshops through media/sales, freelance book editing, web design, help desk, graphic design, online therapies, freelance writing, marketing, film making, translator, and various customer service positions. These positions will all look a little different in terms of time requirements, but they are all perfectly possible in terms of transitioning and making a living while traveling full-time.

Some remote positions will require that you be online at certain times in order to be available to talk to coworkers or clients. This might be some kind of customer service position, or consulting or help desk position, where you need to be online at a certain time in order to be available to take calls and be reached for whatever reason. If you are working with several different clients through freelance work, you may have some individuals who wish to work closely with you through Skype or regular phone calls, while other clients will be happy to hand over the wheel and let you do your thing until it's done. It all depends on the type of work and responsibilities you have. And as we've said, the list of possibilities is endless, so get online and put some hours into researching what you might be interested in doing.

Other income opportunities will require a lot of time investment in order to get to a point where you are actually making money. These are the type of jobs you will probably want to get going well in advance of hitting the road if you intend on making it your full-time income. And the hard reality is, not everyone is successful in making this work. The type of work I'm referring to includes things like writing eBooks to sell online or video workshops and blogging. You're not going to have a ton of followers or readers right at the beginning. It takes time to build an audience, and you need a good size audience in order to start monetizing your product.

A product doesn't have to be a physical item like everything you see at a grocery store. Your product, in this situation, is *you*. As a blogger, you must be able to sell yourself and your knowledge and convince people that what you have to share is worth their time. If you have no platform, this means lots of consistent, quality content and social media development. You may also want to establish an online home base in the form of a Facebook page or a professional, independent website. There is no way to predict just how long it will take to become successful in this arena, and there is no guarantee that you are going to be able to grow an audience to the point where you can sell advertising and monetize your work. That's why it would be highly irresponsible to jump into your RV and hit the road before you've even written your first blog post. It can take several months, and usually much longer than that, to get something like that going.

In the realm of freelance writing, you have a few different options as well, some of them harder to monetize than others. If you have a dream of becoming a professional fantasy book writer, then by all means, put your all into your dream, but don't count on your eBook making a ton of money right away, especially if you have no platform (again). We'll talk about the platform in a minute, but suffice it to say that when you publish independently, it all falls on you to market yourself and get your book in front of readers, as well as getting them interested in actually paying money to read your book. Ebook sales are not a huge moneymaker unless you are selling a ton of them. If you're a writer, you're familiar with how little people actually pay to read an eBook; it can be as little a dollar or two.

So read up on how others monetize and sell their products online, whatever it may be. There are personal trainers who make training videos online and sell monthly subscriptions where people get regular video uploads and personal training advice through email. There are motivational speakers and artists and language teachers and business professionals and therapists and designers all selling their content online and making the money to support a full-time traveling lifestyle. It's possible for you, too. Just do yourself a favor and give yourself lots of time to learn and get established and produce good quality content.

Another option that may be a little more stable in the realm of freelance writing is writing for agencies or clients in the form of blog posts and ghostwriting. This is a more stable and concrete exchange of a service for payment, and you don't have to worry about marketing and selling to readers.

There are quite a few resources online for you to learn from if you are in that limbo of trying to figure out what you want to do on the road. Hopefully, you have some kind of passion or interest that might translate to a mobile situation, and if you're unsure, get online and see if anyone has come up with a creative solution for making your dreams come true.

Making Money Offline

Let's talk about some of the things you can do to make money offline. We're pooling information gathered from lots of different full-time RV-ers, and it's important to recognize that there are risks that come with finding work offline when it comes to meeting new people and arranging temporary work plans.

Again, even when it comes to making money offline, it's been pretty much an agreement across the board from full-time travelers that you will still need internet access to find those offline jobs. Whether it's a work-camping situation or findings odd jobs or temporary jobs in the area where you'll be staying, it's really difficult to find these opportunities quickly without first communicating with potential employers online and responding to job ads.

For the handyman or woman, finding jobs online through craigslist.com is a popular choice, though it is very important to exercise caution when talking and meeting with people online. Craigslist offers a lot of different unique opportunities, whether you're looking for temporary jobs for a week or two to a month or two, or one-off jobs like helping to put up or repair a fence or paint the inside of a home. If you have specific skills in the handyman category, then you can probably find a few things to do to help people out in the area of your campsite. Again, there is a little bit of risk here, and most full-time travelers don't depend solely on jobs like this for their income. There are a lot of situations where one partner works full or part-time online and the other partner goes out and does odd jobs. I'm not saying it can't work to live this way, but you have to consider the possibility that you might be somewhere that doesn't have a lot of job opportunities like this. Then you'd be in a bit of a tight spot.

However, if you plan ahead, you can find temporary jobs that might last a few weeks to a few months. Kinda like the temporary or seasonal jobs, you might have worked as a teenager while you weren't in school. These can be applied for online and interviewed for once you get to a campsite. Then you have a steady temporary income until you're ready to move on to a different campsite. Again, this style of working takes some forethought and you want to have a good idea of what you'll be able to do once you get to that new campsite. It's also a good idea to apply for an interview for a few different positions. That way, you have a backup plan should a position not work out or you decide you hate the work!

Alright, now let's talk about work-camping. Work-camping can be an enjoyable and stable source of income while living in different campsites around the country. Work-camping is simply trading your labor and services for a free campsite, and sometimes even a paycheck. Living rent-free is an incredible perk when it comes to a work-life balance. Rent is often the biggest expense for full-time RV-ers, and fees for staying at different sites often vary quite a bit. Alleviating this source of stress can be a huge factor for financial freedom and living stress-free. But, as with everything else, you'll need to plan and set up this arrangement well in advance of moving to each campsite. You may also be limited in terms of where you can go camp as it will depend on an available work-camping arrangement, if free campsites are required for you to make your full-time traveling life possible. Many full-timers attest to their experience with work-camping as being the only possibility for them to afford the lifestyle. If online work and finding odd jobs are not desirable income options for you, then checking out the world of work-camping is a great alternative.

The benefits of work-camping are many and look a little different for each individual, because the work itself is quite variable. Depending on where you go, you may be doing custodial and maintenance work or maybe working with wildlife and directly with park visitors. There are seasonal opportunities at National Parks for people to come work and live and perform many different duties ranging food prep at a resort to housekeeping to landscaping and construction tasks. And if you're unsure if you would enjoy this type of work and you've got some time to explore before setting out on the road, many of these parks that offer seasonal work opportunities come with dorm housing so you can work and stay right inside the park, just like you would if you were camping there in your RV. This is a great way to see if you would be happy living this kind of lifestyle.

When you're work-camping you'll often be able to stay in one place for a longer period of time and feel comfortable because of the fact that you are not shelling out hundreds of dollars a month on rental fees. This allows for more of a relaxed stable life in the camp, and, if you're making a paycheck on top of that, you'll be able to save up for some of those excursions or big vacation plans that might be more expensive when you're staying somewhere and not working.

You might be asking at this point, "How do I find a work-camping arrangement?" As always, going online and doing your research will reveal lots of resources for finding these opportunities. One of the most popular and biggest sites for this purpose is called workamper.com. This site provides a wealth of knowledge and resources for full-time travelers of all experience levels. Workamper.com is used by job seekers and employers alike and serves as a way to connect them at sites all over the country. For the complete beginner, you will learn all about what work-camping is, what to expect, and the benefits of this working situation. The site offers advice for dos and don'ts when it comes to work-camping and how to appropriately get the ball rolling once you've found a place you're interested in. Don't be afraid to reach out to other seasoned work-campers in order to ask questions and get advice for embarking on this lifestyle. Everyone who has experience in this area will have tips and tricks for making the transition as smooth as possible for you. You'll find links to sign up for newsletters and online magazines which provide an ongoing resource for the latest news in what's going on in the work-camping world as well. The site will also give you the details on what a typical work contract might look like and a checklist for making sure all of the expectations from both sides are clear and in writing. Many employers will actually work with you to choose from a selection of jobs available so that you can find something that you think you would enjoy and be able to perform well.

A lot of times, though, you will find jobs at sites directly from the campground's website, and even see help wanted ads on the grounds itself once you get there, so there really are a lot of different routes to finding work-camping opportunities. And, unless you feel comfortable taking things as they come and living with a bit of uncertainty, it's great to plan ahead and make arrangements with sites before you start your drive there.

Volunteer opportunities and contracting with the government can be another way to find work-camping jobs, but be prepared for a long hiring process, as processing an application for a government entity can take months to go through.

When asked about the biggest challenges of work-camping, seasoned work-campers often cite the sheer unpredictability of the lifestyle. On one hand, many people thrive off of jumping into new experiences and trying new things, but for some, this lifestyle can be a big intimidating simply because of all the unknowns waiting for you. You are working with different people each time you move, you're constantly learning new skills or new ways of doing things. Sometimes you gotta take what's available and it might not be the most amazing job you've ever had. So that's something to consider when you're thinking about work-camping opportunities. Sometimes you'll get a really good explanation beforehand for the expectations and what the job will be like. Other times you might not really even know what you'll be doing until your first day on site and talking to your new employer. As I said, a lot of people find this aspect of the lifestyle exciting and they enjoy the challenge, so if you think you're one of those people, work-camping might be the perfect living situation for you.

Along with unpredictability of job tasks, you will often also not know what your site assignment is going to look like until you get there. Free camping usually means you're not going to be able to pick the perfect site you want from the whole campground, though the opportunities vary from site to site. You will often be assigned a site that you don't get to choose, and if it's not ideal, you'll be living with it for the duration of your contract. So be prepared for this possibility as well.

Another important consideration is what the weather is going to be like in conjunction with whether you are working inside or outdoors. If you're working outside during the summer in an area that gets to be near 100 degrees every day, you're going to want to really prepare yourself for this type of work environment. Investing in comfortable, cool clothing and wearing sunscreen every day are musts, along with constant hydration and breaks in the shade or indoors as often as possible. If the outdoor work in the heat is too much for you, don't be afraid to talk to your employer about it. It's not worth making yourself sick or suffering through if you really can't handle it for the duration of your contract. Most good employers are going to understand and work with you to accommodate your needs.

As you think about working outside in the sunshine on a lovely day out in the park, you might not be thinking about the wildlife and insect population you might have to deal with, so let me be the first one to bring this to your attention! Depending on where you're at and the time of year, you might be dealing with a high population of pests like mosquitoes, chiggers, gnats, etc. The great outdoors comes with them, so you'll need to prepare yourself for it. If you're afraid of snakes, you might do some research and see what kind of snake population exists in the park you're going to be working in. The same goes for spiders. You might be asked to clean or maintain indoor facilities or restrooms out in the park where you likely encounter spiders and lots of bugs. Try to get an idea of what you'll be walking into before your job starts.

With many of the challenges outlined here, there is still an overwhelming consensus from full-time work-campers that they absolutely love doing what they do once they find a good situation and something they enjoy doing. The people you get to meet on the road in these work-camping situations often become lifelong friends, and you may find yourself returning regularly each year to work and camp.

No matter what living and working situations you choose to try, remember to take advantage of the wealth of knowledge and resources available to you online through websites, blogs, YouTube videos and chatting with others who have experience with full-time living and working in an RV.

Chapter 2: Welcome to the Family

In this chapter, we'll talk about some tips and tricks for maximizing your RV experience by helping you with basics from building a campfire to finding the best sites for boondocking. Use this as a resource for what you specifically need to brush up on or learn about as you embark on your full-time RV journey!

Campfires and Cooking

Building a campfire is an essential skill when it comes to camping, and especially for boondocking. If you are unsure how to build a fire, you can go online and look up videos for how to build different types of fires.

Many sites will provide a grill and/or a firepit near your site. Check with the rules of each site concerning fires and firewood. You'll be able to buy bundles of firewood from the campground for building your campfires.

If you are boondocking, we have some advice for building campfires in different environments.

First off, it is very important to make sure you are making fire inside a fire ring that is constructed to keep the fire safe and contained. If you don't have a designated fire ring or stones for the perimeter, you'll want to construct a fire ring that is damp and free of debris and stuff that can catch fire and spread it where you don't want it. Use stones in the area if they are available to help you construct the fire ring. Don't just start the fire in the middle of an area with lots of sticks and grass because you will quickly have an emergency situation on your hands.

Keep water nearby that you can use to put out the fire or contain any fire breaching. You'll need three types of fuel: tinder, kindling and fuel wood. Tinder includes stuff in the environment you can use to catch fire quickly. Things like dry bark, leave and pine needles are good options. If you prefer, you can also use store-bought fire starters.

Kindling is material, most likely small sticks and chunks of wood, which will burn longer and help build your fire up. Finally, fuelwood is going to be those larger logs of wood like those that come with bundles you buy at campsites. Before boondocking, you will want to pre-purchase your fuel wood before heading out to make your life easy. There are also rules to pay attention to which vary according to location concerning what you can gather from the environment for fuelwood.

Perhaps the most common type of fire people build while camping is called the "teepee" and looks just like it sounds. It takes more maintenance than other styles, but it is the easiest to get going. Starting with tinder and kindling, you'll get a small fire going before then positioning larger pieces of wood and fuelwood in a teepee formation, standing on end and leaning against each other. This provides for air passage to fuel the fire, but you'll need to keep an eye on it and reposition as the wood burns down.

Another style is the log cabin fire, and once it's started, needs less maintenance to burn longer. Think of a log cabin where the logs are positioned kind of like Jenga pieces. Use three logs at a time, switching directions as you stack.

Again, this allows for air passage and provides for a more stable formation than the teepee so that you don't have to constantly reposition the fuelwood. This will also give you lots of hot coals for cooking.

When your aim is to cook over your fire, you'll want to construct a fire ring out of rocks or something provided that will be able to support your cooking gear over the fire. So, you might construct a rectangular-looking fire ring if you're laying down a narrow, rectangular grate for cooking purposes, or you might have a large round grate supported by a metal post or other apparatus to keep it in place above your fire.

You can buy special cooking gear for camping, and the assortment of options and styles here is massive, so do some research on what you'd like, but you really don't need anything too fancy. You'll be cooking over the open flame similar to how you would over your gas stove at home, making sure to keep candles away from the flames. You'll have to watch your food closely to make sure you don't burn unintentionally. But boiling water will look the same, of course, so try not to overthink the complexity of cooking over an open flame in the wilderness or wherever it is you've set up to camp. Just remember to keep an eye on your fire and be sure it is contained. Keep cookware handles out of the flames. You can go online to find tips for cooking specific things over your fire, including things like cooking gear recommendations and cooking times for different meats and meal items. The sky is really the limit here for what you can accomplish cooking over a fire, so don't think you're limited to hotdogs and s' mores! You can cook anything from steak and eggs to rice and curry.

Great Boondocking and Free Camping Sites

In this section, we'll let you in on some great destination recommendations for dry camping and boondocking as well as free camping sites.

Hieb City Park in Marion, South Dako̱
park is a beautiful spot that offers free water ̖
electric and is free to camp for up to a week.
There is a nearby city pool.

Clark Canyon Reservoir is located in Dillon,
Montana. There is access right off the interstate
and is a great location on the way to nearby
bigger tourist sites. It is well maintained and
most report a good level of cleanliness.

Blackwell Horse Camp is located in the Hoosier
National Forest in Bloomington, Indiana. This
camp is a spacious area that caters mostly to
people with horses but is open to other campers
as well for free. There are vault toilets in this
area.

Snake River is right outside the southern
entrance to Yellowstone National Park right on
the river. There are lots of different camping
options as you travel along the river. Keep in

limit. There is a ton of space in this area as well, so scout out the area for your rig to find your perfect spot. There is a free dumping spot 8 miles away.

Cebolla Mesa in Questa, New Mexico is located in the Carson National Forest. This is another 14-day stay limit free camping site that overlooks the Rio Grande gorge. Not recommended for rigs over 20 feet long, unless you want to try a tricky route to get to a site.

Craggy Wash in Lake Havasu, Arizona is a great boondocking site on BLM land with a 14-day stay limit. You'll need to check in with camp host here.

Indian Bread Rocks in Bowie Arizona. Another BLM site with a 14-day stay limit with amazing views. Again, bigger rigs might have trouble navigating to get into the site.

Lake Hattie near Laramie, Wyoming is a site near a beautiful lake, if you prefer water sites. There is a 5-day stay limit here.

Jackson Mountain Road is located in Pagosa Springs, Colorado. For an amazing forest and mountain site, this is an excellent choice.

North Creek is located in Virgin, Utah. Another BLM site, this is right outside of Zion National Park with a 14-day stay limit.

Magnolia Beach in Port Lavaca, Texas. Free waterfront camping. Free hot showers nearby! Fine for big rigs, but don't expect much privacy as this is a popular site.

Wedge Overlook in Emery, Utah. BLM land with a 14-day stay limit. Best for rigs 27 feet long and under. One of the most amazing views when it comes to free campsites.

For additional resources and free campsites, compendium.com is a great way to get lots of information and tips for planning out your dry camping adventures. You can also find maps online outlining where exactly the land is in the US that is designated BLM land for boondocking, including the stay limits for each area.

Some things to keep in mind as you look at different free dry camping sites is what resources you're going to need before and during your stay and to plan for that. Some sites have vault toilets and water hookup, others have absolutely nothing nearby for miles. Know whether you're going to need to stop in the nearest town first and stock up on food and water before heading out and know where you'll need to go to dump. In some areas, you'll find amazing campsites, but the nearest town is 20 or more miles away, so keep things like this in mind while you're planning and know how to prepare for your stay.

Traveling with Pets

It's not impossible, or uncommon, to see full-time RV travelers roaming the country along with their pets. If you have a pet, or multiple pets, and are thinking of taking them along on your full-time RV journey, it would be wise to talk to others in the community who also travel with pets to get an idea of the unique challenges doing so is going to present.

The first challenge is, of course, the extra money it's going to take to feed and take care of your pet. Dog food will need to be bought regular just like your own food and will need to be stored, as well as the dog bed, toys, food bowls, and whatever else you keep for your pets. If you are already downsizing quite a bit to fit your life into an RV, you'll have to remember that storing things for your pets' needs is going to cut down on your space even more.

Of course, a lot of people with pets who are getting ready to go on the full-time RV adventure will say that they could no more get rid of their pets than one of their kids. Your pets are part of your family, and if you decide that all of the challenges that come with keeping a pet in an RV are worth it, then it's an easy decision. Just make sure you adequately prepare.

We've compiled a few things to keep in mind after talking to a few travelers who do travel full-time with pets. One of the downsides in addition to living and storage space is that when you are on the road and making stops for shopping and stocking up, etc., you've got to keep an eye on the pets while you're doing so. As couples with pets, one partner will have to stay in the vehicle while the other goes in and gets everything the pair are going to need for the week or for their next camping stay. This can be really inconvenient, as you won't have the freedom to, say, stop somewhere and go into a nice restaurant for a meal because you wouldn't want to leave your pets unsupervised and cooped up in the car.

You might also experience limitations when it comes to excursions for the same reason. Outings around town or even on the campsite become a bit trickier as you have to plan and make sure your pets are safe, and leaving your pets alone in an RV is a little different from leaving them alone in a house. Considerations like keeping the temperature comfortable inside and making sure your pets aren't going to get into anything they shouldn't will be priorities when it comes to going out without the pets. Is your cat or dog going to get anxious cramped up in the tiny space and start eating your only recliner? Just something to think about.

Also, when it comes to traveling full-time with pets, cleaning can become a major chore. If you got a furry animal living inside a small space with you, you're going to be dealing with a lot of pet hair and it will be an endless cycle of getting out the broom or vacuum to get rid of the hair that quickly compounds in such a small space. Remember, too, that animal smells are going to be more intense than in a bigger living space.

Having a separate bedroom in a spacious house or apartment will be a noticeable luxury when you notice how every noise your pets make throughout the day or night is inescapable for you, living together in an RV.

RV Clubs and Campground Memberships

Campground clubs like Passport America offer frequent and full-time campers a way to save on campsites all over the country. The basic structure is that you pay a yearly fee, and in exchange, you'll be able to camp at participating campground for a discount. This comes in handy and most users have expressed that the membership fee pays for itself within the first time you use it. There are a few exceptions, like high tourist seasons and holidays, when the discount won't apply.

The website and app provide a detailed map to point out all of the participating campgrounds by state. The site will also give you all the details you need, like contact info and amenity details.

Something to keep in mind with Passport America is that every campground is going to be slightly different in terms of their discount policy. You'll need to do some research and contact the campground ahead of time to double check your rate before staying there. Some campgrounds will give you a discount for one or two night, while others will apply the discount to a month-long stay. As mentioned above, some high tourist season dates will be blacked for these discounts, so you'll need to double check to see if you're going to be able to get those discounts during times of the year when the place is super busy, or around the holiday. Some campgrounds also have additional fees for pets and other things, so you'll definitely have to check out the place before you stay there to make sure you're not going to get hit with extra fees you weren't expecting.

Thousand Trails is another campground membership option. The contracts for a membership package with Thousand Trails are more complex and you will need to take time to read through and really understand what you're getting with your membership.

There are several packages to choose from with more or less features reflected in prices. Features of membership packages include booking in advance from 60 days to 180 days. But the different packages come with different benefits, so if you decide to look into a membership with them, do your research and learn the ins and outs of each membership package.

Another membership option is RPI, which functions similarly to other memberships with a smaller pool of participating parks.

Good Sams is another campground membership offering a smaller stay discount at parks across the US. The discount is only 10% as opposed to the 50% discount you get with Passport America (current as of spring 2019).

The important area to do your homework in when it comes to campground memberships is studying the maps of participating campgrounds across the country. Many full-time RV-ers decide to purchase more than one campground membership, so it's important to make sure that you are adding value by doing so and not purchasing a membership that is basically full of overlap in terms of participating parks.

Joining some kind of campground membership is highly recommended by most of the full-time RV-ers I've talked to, and many of them are very simple to get started with, especially Passport America. As mentioned earlier, the membership pays for itself within just a few nights, so it's definitely something to consider while you're looking for ways to save money on the road. Thousand Trails offers packages for both part-time campers and full-timers who might be interested in staying at nicer resort-style campgrounds around the country. There are lots of rules and regulations to read over before signing a contract for their more expensive packages, but it can be a great way to save money and stay at some amazing places for those full-timers who are willing to invest money upfront for the year instead of paying a few weeks or a month at a time. Be sure to take your time to plan carefully and make sure you are adhering to the rules outlined in your specific membership, as they require you to stay only a limited amount of days before moving to a new park, and this requirement varies in length depending on the level of membership you purchase.

Planning Driving Routes

When it comes to planning out your driving route between campsites, the first thing you'll need to nail down is your point A and point B destinations. Know where you're coming from and where you're going. As we discussed in earlier chapters, plan to travel at a speed of around 60 mph in a bigger rig for safety reasons. And remember rule number one when it comes to the full-time RV traveling lifestyle: Take your time!

Once you have a starting point and end point, you will need to plan how you're going to get there. You want to make sure, depending on the type and size of your RV, that your route is clear of any roadways or obstacles that are going to cause a problem for you. There are apps available and the website allstays.com has a tool you can use to look on your route and see if there are any low tunnel or bridge clearances or things like road weight limits, etc. You'll want to avoid any particularly windy roads or roads that are going to cause undue stress on whoever is driving your rig, especially if you've got a giant fifth wheeler. The allstays app is available for a fee and provides RV-specific travel info and navigation tools to warn you about safe routes and routes unsuitable for your RV as well as speed limits and recommendations.

The next consideration is where you're going to stop between long drives. Allstays is a good resource for this as well, giving you up-to-date information on larger truck stop and areas that are appropriate for RVs to stop, park and/or fill up. In addition, use apps specific to finding rest stops on the road to give you all the options available on your route.GasBuddy is another app available for searching for available gas stations along your route for both gas and diesel as well as current prices.

Keep in mind that if you are trying to calculate how long it's going to take you to get to your next destination and are using Google maps, the travel time is going to be different because you will be traveling more slowly than the speed Google uses to calculate travel time, so just keep that in mind so that you're not on the road and shocked as you pull in to your new campsite at a way later time than your phone told you it would be.

The next consideration for traveling between sites is what time of day (or night) you're going to leave. This can make a huge difference in terms of how long it takes you based on traffic and how close you are to big metropolitan areas where people are commuting to and from work from outside the city. This may prompt some adjustment in your route in order to avoid high traffic times, if possible. Driving your RV through a city or highly populated area with lots of traffic can be very stressful and sometimes dangerous if you are not super confident in your driving skills or are in the first year of driving your new RV. Things like pivot points and tail swing become a huge factor when you have lots of traffic around you and have to navigate lots of turns through a city, so keep these factors in mind when you are traveling your route. Taking a longer route may be a safer and less stressful option if you can avoid areas like this, even though it will mean arriving a little later to your ultimate destination. If you have to drive through the city, try to plan to be going through during non-rush-hour times.

Making the Most of Your Free Time

Let's take a breath and talk about some lighter tips and tricks that have to do with making the best of your time at your camp destinations.

YouTubers Keep Your Daydream offer lots of videos and ideas for how to maximize your enjoyment when it comes to your free time. One of their biggest tips for fitting everything you want to do into each of your camp stays is simply to make a list when you're planning your stay. It's easy to get overwhelmed with the planning aspect when you look at a campsite and see all of the available activities nearby, so once you've figured out the logistics and have the financial part of things addressed, then you can breathe a bit and set aside some time to make a list of the things you want to do in your free time while you are there. Keep in mind how long you're going to be staying in one location and don't try to do absolutely everything there is to do if you're only going to be there a few days or a few weeks. You can always come back next year!

Try not to focus on the stuff you're not going to have time for and focus on the things you're planning to do. As I said, you're not going to have time or money to do everything there is to do in the area, but you absolutely some fabulous evenings and weekends. You don't have to fit every single thing in. Be sure to budget and balance what things you can go out and do for free, like hiking, and what things are going to cost a bit of money, like admission to a waterpark or renting skis. Don't forget to account for food expenses as well, as part of your free time enjoyment might include a restaurant that you really want to go to for a special Friday night date.

Another tip for making your free time memorable while on the road is to simply document your experiences, whether it's through videos you upload onto YouTube or writing in a journal and taking pictures for a scrapbook. You'll be happy you did so later on as you look back on what you've been able to do and see and experience. I've seen a lot of full-time RV-ers who put up fun maps of the US and mark each city or state with fun stickers or colors as they go to remind them of where they've been and where they want to go.

RV-ing in Europe!

Yes, there is absolutely an RV community in Europe, and travelers regular RV across Europe seeing some of the most amazing sites in the world in a whole new way.

There are some interesting differences between American RVs and European RVs. One big difference here is that there are pretty much no generators in European RVs. One reason for this is the fact that the European manufacturers are trying to keep the weights down for these RVs because going over a certain weight puts you in a CDL category where drivers need a special license to drive it. European RVs also tend to not house the typical powered appliances like microwaves that are virtually ubiquitous in America. You'll see propane ovens, but microwaves are not as much of a thing over in Europe as they are here.

Another noticeable difference between European RV lifestyle and American RV lifestyle reported by RV-ers traveling across Europe is that there doesn't seem to be as much concern with connectivity. You don't see things like cell boosters at RV shows. There is a marked cultural difference that speaks for the RV experience being a time to get away from the way people usually live in their "normal" day-to-day lives, so the big emphasis in Europe is not on comfort and basically recreating a home life that is similar in capability to a sticks and bricks home, but on experiencing an unplugged, different experience of the world and in new destinations. The European RV experience tends toward more of the weekend warrior type thing you see in America, with an emphasis on shorter stays and really getting out and enjoying what the scenery and environment have to offer. You don't see a lot of Europeans in campgrounds walking around with cell phones or on laptops as you do in the US. A big part of that is because America is full of full-time RV-ers who are working remotely and making a living on the road, so there is an absolute necessity in being connected, unlike in European RV campgrounds. That's not to say it doesn't exist over there, but it is far more popular in America.

Another trend in European RVs is acrylic windows. This is interesting in that it offers a whole new level of soundproofing, so that if you are camped close by lots of neighbors, you get a kind of added layer of privacy in that you don't have to hear what's going on around you quite as much. They also help with temperature control inside the RV, keeping the cold out in the winter and the heat in during the winter.

There are also RVs in Europe with manual transmissions, which is pretty much unheard of in America. It is becoming more and more common to encounter young people today who have never driven a car with manual transmission, but this is not the case in Europe. You will also find that the RVs in Europe are built to provide a lot more space in the "garage" area for various toys. We have toy haulers here in the US, but unless you invest in a large RV with space specifically added for things like a motorcycle or ATV, you usually end up with an RV with a limited amount of storage space. This is another reflection of the cultural difference between US RV-ers and European RV-ers in terms of treating the RV experience as a vacation with an emphasis on the outdoors and doing things you don't usually get to do in normal day-to-day work life. And this isn't just in the bigger RVs in Europe, even the smaller RVs will reserve lots of space for gear.

With that said, the RVs, in general, are simply smaller, as just about everything infrastructurally seems to be. You see smaller roadways throughout European countries as opposed to the giant road and highways you see in America. So you simply don't have room for the giant, heavy RVs you see in America. When you're traveling around Europe, perhaps going through smaller towns, you really can't be in something huge like an American class A motorhome, for example. There are really some fascinating differences to be found between American style and European style RVs.

Chapter 3: Modern Rv Living

RV living has been a fascinating facet of American culture for years, but it has started, over the last decade, to really pick up steam in terms of attracting younger generations of travelers to the full-time RV lifestyle. Camping has been a popular pastime for decades but living full-time on the road is something many people would have laughed at just a few short years ago, and many still do. I hear from individuals all the time who share their plans with loved ones or parents or adult children only to get a reaction that seems to question their sanity.

The growth in popularity of this lifestyle points to a much bigger picture and trend in America, and it is a reflection of the fact that many people, both young and older, are growing tired of the rat race that has been prescribed for them and their parents and their parents before them. There is a massive change on the horizon that is growing towards a different picture of American life and work. We can see that clearly through the explosion of online work opportunities and the number of people who decide right out of college to make their own way, creating their own businesses from scratch. The idea of the cycle life being dictated by a life-long corporate career behind a desk are quickly becoming old-fashioned. People change jobs often, sometimes many times, before finding something that they really love. Many young people today start out on a corporate trajectory or in a position with a big company only to find that they are not feeling fulfilled or getting the satisfaction from their work that they once thought they would get. As our capitalist economy grows in a way that separates those who have away from those who have-not, we start to see how easy it is for the average worker to be completely overlooked in favor of squeezing out every last ounce of energy for as little money and benefits as possible. It's just no longer something that everyone wants. The American dream is changing in big ways. The old one has all but disappeared.

The minimalist movement has grown and continues to grow in conjunction with the green movement, advocating for a new way of life that emphasizes the quality of life, health, and conservation instead of mass consumerism and self-destruction. It has become too easy for people to fall into a pit of debt and even poverty early in life as expenses for housing and interest rates for college loans bury young people who have not even embarked on a career yet. Many people find out too late that those degrees they once thought were essential have nothing to do with what they actually want to do with their lives, which they only discover through actually living and experiencing life. The growing minimalism and RV lifestyle movement is a massive statement regarding the passion and desire people have for setting themselves free and experiencing what life has to offer. They've decided that daily misery at a job they hate for the payoff of maybe a week or two out of the year for a vacation is absurd and incredibly limiting. There is so much more out there to discover and experience!

Learning to live according to minimalism principles is a great way to help you transition to the mindset that you will need to live successfully in an RV full time. The concept is quite simple, and most people who adopt the lifestyle attest to the many financial, mental, physical, and even spiritual benefits they've experienced as a result.

Minimalism

Set aside some time to sit down and get out a journal and something to write with, or alternatively, your laptop. Start by writing a little about what it is about your life and your possessions that you find difficult to change. What scares you about making a lifestyle change? What do you think you would miss? How do you think you would handle these changes emotionally? What does your partner or family think? Do you believe a lot of your mindset stems from the values that were passed down from your parents?

Our possessions often harbor an emotional attachment that insulates us and makes us feel cozy, even when their utility is zero or next to zero. When you find it hard to let go of something, there is often some kind of emotional hold the item has over you for one reason or another. Perhaps you hold on to photos of your mother who has passed, or you just can't let go of that old prom dress because you kissed your husband for the first time while wearing it. These attachments make sense, but part of the minimalist lifestyle adheres to a principle of assigning meaning to experiences rather than objects. The objects themselves hold no intrinsic value or utility in a lot of cases, we simply assign them value based on our emotional responses. Once we can learn to associate living and life experiences with meaning and value instead of objects, we can start to open up a whole new world that is free from stuff that weighs us down. Oftentimes you won't even realize that all your stuff is weighing you down until you get rid of it or donate it or give it to somebody who will actually find a use for it. Clutter is like a blanket we secure over ourselves, and it can be tough to start to let that go, but the result from successfully doing so is absolutely priceless and life-changing.

One of the biggest challenges to transitioning to a minimalist lifestyle is fear. Somewhere in the back of your mind, you know that if you're not surrounded by distractions and media devices and chores and things to take care of that you will have to face yourself and think about life in a new way. With all of that clutter out of the way, you will have nowhere to escape, and that is really what it's all about. Once you get out of your own way, you will discover new values that have the breathing room to extend away from yourself. It won't be all about you and what makes you comfortable anymore. You will start to actually see the world and the people around and notice how your behaviors and connections impacts others.

Consumerism and surrounding yourself with stuff and distraction is directly related to a poor lifestyle in terms of your health. When we get lazy with our lives and our thoughts processes, hiding from the fact that we are tired and hate our jobs or current life situations, we don't have the energy to care about what we are putting into our bodies, let alone getting plenty of healthy exercises. When you have all that stress weighing you down, the last thing you want to spend your energy on is taking care of your health, which is exactly what you really need. Minimalists often talk about how benefits such as healthy lifestyle changes have gone hand in hand with a progression towards this new lifestyle as they start to realize the importance of taking care of the health of, not only their own bodies, but of the world around them.

Nothing ignites a passion for taking care of the earth and conservationism like living full-time in an RV. When you hit the road and start to see the immense beauty and breathtaking views that exist in our country, it is impossible not to feel a new sense of connection with the environment and with the earth. There exists now a ton of research documenting the real, tangible mental health benefits that follow from simply being out in nature, and there is really no drug that can replace that feeling.

You don't have to wait until you are living full-time in an RV to experience this transformation.

After you've written about your personal feelings about your lifestyle and possessions, start a new paragraph and write about what you dream your life would look like if you didn't feel stressed all the time. What exactly are the elements in your life causing you stress? Are they things you have any control over? Are there changes you could make to alleviate this stress? How much effort are you willing to put into making a change?

As you write, start to notice where your big trigger points are where you start to feel more anxious or afraid. These are the things which need to be addressed, and I understand they may not be things you have control over. However, I know that there are things you can start doing today to start the process of freeing yourself and moving toward a minimalist and healthier lifestyle, if it's something you are ready to do.

A first challenge you might consider is cutting down on your wardrobe items (yes, ladies, that includes shoes!). See if you can whittle down your wardrobe and sell or donate at least half of the clothes that you currently own. How does this make you feel? Did you instantly get a feeling like it would be impossible to do? Try examining this feeling. Why do you feel that way? What makes you think you actually need all that clothing? If you can't think of a good reason, that's because there is none!

If you can get past this challenge, you are well on your way. Think about the stuff you've held on to that you hardly even acknowledge. Do you have stuff stored in your garage or in your closets that you haven't even looked at in years? Why do you still have these things? The key in this process is to look around and really think about and question what service these things are providing for your life. If you can't come up with anything, then it goes in the donate/sell pile.

As you get rid of more and more stuff, remember to keep a journal to record the feelings you go through. There is no wrong way to feel during this process, and some people are going to have a harder time emotionally than others. And that's perfectly fine! We are all unique and we all have unique struggles and emotional hang-ups to work through. Just remember that life is short, and if you don't start addressing these things now, they might just hang around forever and prevent you from taking a risk and going for the life you truly want.

We can see the effects of holding on to stuff and the power of clutter when we observe the opposite extreme to minimalism that exists in American society, and that is chronic hoarding.

Chronic hoarding is not just a bad habit of hanging on to things. Those with real, chronic hoarding issues have often gone through traumatic experiences that have led them to seek refuge from the emotional turmoil through buying and storing things. This process works as a sort of insulator, keeping them from having to experience the full brunt of those emotions all the time. When they have layers and layers of things working as an obstacle to them and their feelings, then they have a way to protect themselves from very painful thought processes. This, of course, is a destructive course of action because the problem tends to get worse and worse as time goes on and these individuals avoid addressing the root of their emotional problems. Very rarely would you find someone who identifies as a hoarder but also as someone with zero anxiety or emotional stress.

Oftentimes, individuals with this particular issue will go through something called cognitive behavioral therapy in order to get past the harmful emotional attachments that they've affixed to their things. The process is a slow one and can be very painful for the individual who is suffering. But the more they work through the real reasons they're hanging on to things, the more they start to feel those emotional burdens lifting, and that's what it's all about: setting themselves free.

Of course, I'm not calling anyone reading this book a hoarder, by any means. But it is important to understand that having lots of things and feeling attachment for them is not the end-all-be-all decider for whether or not you can transition to an RV lifestyle. Transitions and changes are difficult for anyone, and if you wait until you feel 100% ready and confident and without fear, then you will definitely never go out and buy that RV.

Go back to that journal and start envisioning how you think you feel on the road in an RV and living the lifestyle. How much stuff are you willing to let go of in order to work toward making that dream a reality? Imagine yourself going through the garage or your house and assign a value to each item. Are these numbers anywhere near as high as the value of that experience and feeling of being free and creating an intentional, purpose-driven life on the road full of adventure? Probably not!

Consider talking to family and loved ones about your dream, but don't let other people convince you that what you want out of life is impossible or impractical. Most people who feel no desire to change or do not understand the lifestyle often react negatively when they hear someone talking about wanting to sell the house and everything they own to get an RV and hit the road. It's true, it sounds quite crazy when most people live in a stable environment working a 9 to 5. But if you know you're not happy with this arrangement, then you deserve the prospect of a different life. One that offers more in just about every way you can imagine.

Remember, there are a ton of resources online for you to tap in to, and lots of people in the RV community who will be so excited to hear from someone who is interested in the transition to RV life. Just going through and watching a few YouTube videos will show you just how excited this community is to reach out and connect and share the knowledge they've gained from their lives on the road. Consider talking to one of them and sharing your feelings if you are still on the fence and wondering if you have what it takes. Odds are, most of the people you talk to will have gone through exactly what you're going through.

Online Resources

There are some amazing YouTubers/bloggers who have been full-time RV traveling for at least a year and release regular videos about their lives on the road, including instructional videos for absolutely anything you'd want to learn about RV life.

Keep Your Daydream. These YouTubers have created many, many videos on the subject of living full-time in an RV, and they also travel with kids. Check out their videos for a whole lot of entertaining and incredibly helpful content, whether you are brand new to the scene or looking to connect with others in the community.

Another top-of-the-list YouTuber couple in terms of video quality and entertainment value is EnoyTheJourney.Life. This is a couple who travel without kids in a larger fifth wheel RV. They have shared so much about their experiences and what they've learned on the road, and I highly recommend you check out their videos.

Some other YouTuber/bloggers to check out include:

CreativityRV
AStreaminLife

Drivin' and Vibin'

RV Odd Couple

Four Life Adventures

You, Me & the RV

Tim and Fin

Chickery's Travels

WildOnTheGo

You will find many more as you search for additional content and resources and/or blogs sharing content all about full-time RV living. Just Google "full-time RV living" or go to YouTube and search for anything you'd like to know about transitioning to the RV life!

Sites/apps for RV-ers:

Allstays.com and app

Compendium.com

RV Parky

RV Buddy

Gas Buddy

Passportamerica.com

Thousandtrails.com

Workamper.com

Coolworks.com

Workers on wheels

Livingthedream.com

Uscampgrounds.info

Sanidump.com

Overnightrvparking.com

If you want, go on iG and follow:

Gorving

Camper.lifestyle

Vanlifedistrict

Vanlifeisawesome

Project.vanlife

Conclusion

Thank you for making it through to the end of *RV Living*, let's hope it was informative and able to provide you with all of the tools you need to achieve your goals whatever they may be.

You now have a great foundation of knowledge for moving forward toward your goals of making the dream of RV living a reality. I hope that by reading about some of the amazing things RV living has to offer that you have moved a little closer to your decision to make the transition. I hope that I've given you the tools you need to help build your confidence that this is possible for just about anyone, no matter their current living situation. If you have the will and physical ability to make it work, then there is really nothing to stop you, except your own doubts. Again, I strongly encourage that you go out there and meet others who have made the transition before you so that you can continue learning and getting a taste of what it really means to live full-time in an RV.

There is no substitution for experience when it comes to learning about this lifestyle, so see about renting an RV for whatever amount of time is feasible for you so that you can see for certain if this lifestyle is something you want. It's not for everyone, but I think that it could be perfect a lot of people who previously thought they could never achieve such a thing. My goal in writing this book was to convince each and every one of my readers that it is very possible, and that you should consider doing it sooner rather than later. You never know what's going to happen down the road, and you don't want to wait until it's too late!

You've learned about the basics of RV living, the tools and recommended equipment you'll need before leaving on your first trip, and the pros and cons of RV living. You've learned about the options you have for making a living on the road through working remotely, starting an online business or working as a freelancer. You know about boondocking and several options for free camping that can be found all over the country.

You've also learned the basics of the different types of RVs available to buy. You've got a taste of what it might be like to live in an RV with pets and how you might be able to find work in a work-camping situation.

You know how to build a proper campfire have started feeling the excitement of what could lay in store for you should you take the leap and buy that RV.

Now it's time for you to start taking your knowledge and applying to your own preparations. If you've decided you absolutely cannot continue on with your life without prepping for that inevitable transition, then you now know what you need to do to start making that dream a reality. Do your research, put time into planning, and educate yourself to the best of your ability to that you experience a few unpleasant surprises as possible when you're on the road. Learn from others' mistakes, and don't be afraid to learn from your own. Because you are definitely going to make a mistake or two. It might be a rocky start, but you're not alone, and you will be joining a growing community full of vibrant, enthusiastic people you can now call friends and part of your RV "tribe." Document the ride from the beginning, and you will have years of memories to look back on and remember as you feel the pride of finally having been able to make the best decision of your life.

There is an innate sense of adventure and discovery that comes with RV life. Many full-time RV-ers talk about how RV living changed them on a fundamental and personal level, and for the better. When you live full-time on the road, you may learn to let go of many things about your personality which hold you back and are not conducive to this lifestyle.

One of the most consistent tips I hear from RV-ers is *take your time...*

Thanks Again
Michael

Made in the USA
Coppell, TX
17 May 2020